HAS GOD PROVEN
HIS EXISTENCE?

HAS GOD PROVEN HIS EXISTENCE?

BY

DR. HAROLD R. EBERLE

Worldcast Publishing
Yakima, Washington, USA

HAS GOD PROVEN HIS EXISTENCE?

© 2019 BY DR. HAROLD R. EBERLE
FIRST PRINTING JUNE 2019

WORLDCAST PUBLISHING
P. O. BOX 10653
YAKIMA, WA 98909-1653
(509) 248-5837
WWW.WORLDCASTMINISTRIES.COM
OFFICE@WORLDCASTMINISTRIES.COM

ISBN 1-882523-49-0
COVER BY CHRIS RITCHIE

Table of Contents

Introduction

There is a system of thought that influences people in the Western world to distance them from God—even remove God from their mind and heart.

That system of thought influences everyone in the Western world to some degree, but it took an especially firm grip on the minds of the educated in Europe throughout the early-to-mid 20th century. That contributed to a mass exodus of people from the churches, leaving the European Church withered and subdued. Now in North America, a similar system of thought is being imposed upon the minds of young people through social media, books, songs, movies, television, and, most importantly, our educational system.

The results are most evident at institutions of higher learning. A large percentage of students enter into these environments believing in God but emerge as atheists (people who believe God does not exist) or agnostics (people who do not know if God exists). A transformation of their thoughts takes place during those four or more years that puts their life on a different course.

A similar transformation takes place in the minds of people who never attend a university but keep up with the same general thought patterns through their own reading or by following the opinions of others who are in step with current thought patterns in Western society.

Introduction

As a result, there is another falling away taking place throughout the Western world, especially where I live in the United States. Thousands of young adults have abandoned their faith. A close friend of mine who once was a pastor now tells me he is an atheist. Even closer to home is the fact that I briefly became an agnostic after attending a seminary. I went into the seminary hoping to learn about God but came out not knowing if God exists. I have since worked through that episode in my life and now am a firm believer in God.

I am writing to provide sound, logical thought to help stop the falling away. I hope everyone who reads this book will benefit, but my target audience consists of the younger adults who are now being inundated with a system of thought that bends their mind toward atheism / agnosticism.

I also hope to provide leaders with the understanding they need to equip young adults before they go off to universities or other environments where their minds will be assaulted with ideas supporting a worldview without God. To help leaders provide that support, this book can be used as a teaching manual, with questions for discussion provided in Appendix B.

• • •

This book is written in five sections. Each section is broken into points, and each point presents one clear thought. As a result, you will find this book an easy read.

Section 1 traces the God-diminishing progression of thought that developed among Western philosophers over the course of the last 2,400 years. A parallel progression typically develops in the mind of those who move from theism (belief in God) to atheism (belief there is no God) or agnosticism (belief that no one knows if God exists). I hope readers will recognize if that progression has taken root in their own thought processes.

Others will simply identify the progression so they can resist it taking root in their minds and the minds of their loved ones.

Although we will be tracing the negative path of philosophical thought, this is not meant to be a criticism of all the philosophers who have lived and worked to further our understanding. There have been many God-loving philosophers throughout history. To them, we should be grateful. However, there have also been philosophers who have used their skills at logical thinking to create a path for others to follow into darkness, away from God.

Section 2 of this book identifies the values of people who have embraced the historic Western philosophical progression. A brief description of those values will open your eyes to see why today's society is changing so rapidly. You will also see where many of your own ideas originated. Right now, you may think your own values are your own, but Section 2 will show you how many of those values have been absorbed from the atheistic/agnostic worldview of those around you.

Section 3 corrects the God-diminishing progression of thought by:

1. Exposing two false assumptions lying at its foundation
2. Proposing two concepts to replace those false assumptions, concepts that produce to an entirely different progression of thought leading to theism

In **Section 4**, we will develop and contrast two definitions of faith. The first definition corresponds with philosophical thought. The second definition corresponds with an understanding developed from the Bible.

Understanding these differences is essential before reading Section 5.

Introduction

In **Section 5**, we will examine the evidence / proof for or against the existence of God. Our goal is to determine which progression of thought leads to truth. We will see why it is more logical to believe in God than to not believe. Our end goal is to provide a logical progression of thought leading to theism.

• • •

A glossary is located in Appendix A at the back of this book.

• • •

I am not a professional philosopher. My expertise is in theology and Western history which I have studied and taught for over 40 years. Professional philosophers will see my explanations of their field of study as over-simplified. Although I have read many of the writings of the noted historic philosophers, my awareness of them is as an observer who considers how their thoughts influenced my own fields of study in theology and history.

• • •

The pronoun "he" will be used when referring to God but this is not meant to determine the gender of God. The related issues are simply beyond the scope of the discussions in this book.

SECTION ONE

Progression of Thought
Leading to Atheism/Agnosticism

We are about to trace the dominant progression of philosophical thought that developed within Western civilization
over the last 2,400 years. It is a progression that leads people
into atheism/agnosticism.

The reason we must have this discussion is because the
thoughts of the philosophers play a major role in determining
the direction of society. We are part of society. Without knowing
it, we are being directed. Most people are unaware that this
is happening. They think their thoughts are solely their own
and they don't like to be told otherwise. Of course, we each
have glimmers of inspiration from time to time, but the major
thoughts that establish the course of civilization have been laid
out by others. People in positions of influence have thought our
most life-forming thoughts decades before we did.

Many of those original thinkers are the philosophers sitting
in their private offices, reading and writing scholarly books.
They will emerge from time to time to teach in a university
classroom or to engage in discussions with their academic
peers, but their primary work is done sitting in an easy chair,
thinking about the future—where society will be one hundred
or more years from now.

Progression of Thought Leading to Atheism/Agnosticism

Those philosophers are crafting ideas that will build upon each other, developing a whole progression of thought leading to a predetermined destination. Their crafted ideas will serve as words of a prophet only to be fulfilled by succeeding generations. Their words not only predict the future but also help to create it.

The thoughts of the philosophers filter down to the masses. Phrase-by-phrase, people incorporate those thoughts into their daily lives. As they do, the masses move further down the path which has been pioneered and paved by the philosophers. Eventually the masses arrive at the same finish line that the philosophers crossed long ago.

From time to time, it is good to step away and acquire a broader perspective. Then the person on the journey can see where the path is leading.

That is the goal of the first section of this book—to step back and see where the historic Western philosophical path has carried humanity and where it is leading us. Once you read this section, you will understand how the Western philosophical progression of thought leads to atheism/agnosticism. After you see it, you can decide if you want to stay on that path to its end.

Point 1.1: Philosophy and Epistemology

Philosophy is not hard to understand. The word, "philosophy" simply means "love of wisdom." We are all philosophers because we all accumulate knowledge in many areas and try to make sense of the world.

Philosophy can be broken into several areas of wisdom, including theology, humanity, politics, ethics, economics, mathematics, physics, etc., but there is one overarching area philosophers have been discussing for over 2,400 years. It is called "epistemology." It focuses on the question, "How can we be certain that what we think is true?"

In an effort to make epistemology easy to understand, let me offer a story of two coworkers having an epistemological discussion about the weather forecast. Oscar told Harley that the news media predicted a severe storm would pass through their region on the following day. What made the ensuing discussion an epistemological discussion had nothing to do with the subject matter of the storm, but rather whether or not they could know for sure if the forecast was accurate. Their discussion went as follows:

Oscar: "The weather reporter said a severe storm will hit our region tomorrow."

Harley: "Do you trust the weather reporter?"

Oscar: "Well, I have seen her be accurate on many occasions. So, I do pay attention to what she says."

Harley: "Have you ever actually kept track of how many times she gets it right and how many times she gets it wrong?"

Oscar: "No, but several other weather reporters are predicting the same storm."

Harley: "How do you know those reporters aren't all repeating the same report from one weather forecaster?"

Oscar: "I guess I don't know but there must be some truth to all of those reports because the mayor put out a warning for everyone to stay home tomorrow."

Harley: "I remember when the mayor gave the same warning last year and nothing happened. Don't you remember that?"

Oscar: "Well, I guess you are right. We can't be sure if the storm will come."

Oscar and Harley were involved in a philosophical discussion, and more specifically, in an epistemological discussion. They were trying to figure out if the storm was really going to happen. They wanted to know if they could be sure.

That is what an epistemological discussion is. Everyone has them at some time. It is simply a discussion to discover what is really true.

Point 1.2: Socrates and Epistemology

Socrates

In ancient Greece, Socrates (c. 469–399 BC) was the first, most well-known philosopher to lay down the fundamentals of epistemology.

Socrates became famous for publicly asking difficult questions of other leaders in his community. When a leader would make some public statement, Socrates would ask one question after another until he revealed any false assumptions or contradictions in their logic. Once those assumptions or contradictions were revealed, everyone listening could see why the original statements were true or false.

Many philosophers followed in the footsteps of Socrates. As they did, they discussed some of the most fundamental questions facing humanity, such as:

1. Does God exist?

2. What is the nature of man?

3. What is right and what is wrong?

4. What is the meaning of life?

As these fundamental questions of life were addressed, epistemology continued as the overarching work of the philosophers. With every question, the philosophers honed their skills at distinguishing truth from error.[1] For those philosophers, logic was the primary tool of their craft. They purposely tried to reject any idea that could not be proven logically.

Point 1.3: Foundation Laid by Plato

Plato

After Socrates, his disciple Plato (c. 427–347 BC) came to the forefront. Plato contributed many ideas, but the most important for our discussion here is that he offered a "cosmology" for all the Western world.

---

1 Because the early philosophers came to many wrong conclusions, some readers who are familiar with the work of the ancient philosophers may take exception to this idea that they honed their skills. In some cases, they merely argued or came into agreement concerning what they would accept as true.

Progression of Thought Leading to Atheism/Agnosticism

Cosmology refers to one's understanding of the origin and nature of the world. For example, a modern scientist may have a cosmology of the world beginning with a big bang from which the whole universe came into existence about 13.7 billion years ago. An example of another cosmology is Christians who believe Genesis 1 literally and, therefore, that God created the world by speaking it into existence a few thousand years ago.

Plato's cosmology was different than both of those. It consisted of two worlds, a spiritual world that always existed and a natural world that was created. Because it consisted of two worlds, Plato's cosmology is considered "dualistic."

Plato believed humans can access the spiritual world through their thoughts, so if they meditate on perfect things, they are actually reaching into and experiencing the perfect things in the spiritual world.

PLATO: DUALISTIC COSMOLOGY

Most people in the Western world today are influenced by Plato's dualist cosmology to some degree. They tend to think of a spiritual world (heaven) being both separate from and located above the natural world.

Point 1.4: The Foundation Altered by Aristotle

Aristotle

Plato had a disciple named Aristotle (384–322 BC), who built on the cosmology of Plato, but he added God to the picture. This is in contrast to Plato who simply thought of god[2] as whatever encompasses all of the perfect thoughts in his spiritual world. Aristotle referred to God as the "Prime Mover" or "Immoveable Mover" giving his God credit for pushing the natural world into existence. Aristotle saw the Prime Mover as immovable because it seemed logical that any being able to push the natural world into existence must be big enough to not be moved.

ARISTOTLE:
GOD AS THE IMMOVABLE MOVER

Point 1.5: The Development of a Progression of Thought

Western philosophers built on the fundamental ideas of Socrates, Plato, and Aristotle, altering what they considered

---

2 I will not be capitalizing the word "god," when referring to a god who is impersonal as a force, power, or truth.

unfounded and adding what they saw as the next logical step in the progression of philosophical thought.

Those progressions of thought are still developing today. They exist primarily as dialogs going on among the educated elite, either face-to-face or indirectly through their books and lectures. When some noted professor makes a public philosophical statement, others either attack or defend it. A philosophical statement should stand or fall depending upon its logical integrity. A philosophical statement that stands over time will continue to be discussed, and therefore, influence others who think philosophically.

Today, similar progressive dialogs are going on in almost every field of study, including politics, medicine, education, business, religion, psychology, engineering, music, art, etc. In almost every field, there is a progression of thought that influences the future within that field.

However, our interest here is in the Western philosophical progression of thought. That progression has been developing for over 2,400 years, and it is the progression that is currently leading multitudes into atheism or agnosticism.

Point 1.6: Christianity Spreads Across the Roman Empire

For the first three centuries AD, Christians were persecuted and Christianity existed as a subculture within the Roman Empire. Then in 313 AD, Emperor Constantine passed a law granting religious freedom. Soon Christianity became the official religion of the Roman Empire, and several million people flooded into the Church. Facilitating this sudden and

Augustine

12

massive expansion of Christianity were Church leaders and most influential among them was Augustine (354–430 AD).

Augustine built his theology upon Plato's dualistic cosmology with two worlds, the spiritual world and the natural world. However, by Augustine's time, the spiritual world was referred to as "heaven" and the God of the Bible was seen as dwelling in heaven.

AUGUSTINE:
SPIRITUAL AND NATURAL WORLD, WITH GOD DWELLING IN HEAVEN

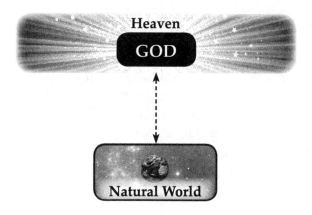

Augustine's understanding of faith was also significant for the developing progression of philosophical thought. As a teacher of Christian thought, Augustine wanted people to know that faith in God was necessary to become a Christian, and he saw the Church as the keeper and proclaimer of the truths about God. This developed into the understanding that people must accept what the Church teaches in order to become a Christian.

For modern people, this type of dependency upon the Church may sound archaic, but it is helpful to remember that the vast majority of people in Augustine's time could not read, and so, dependency upon the Church was much more reasonable. That dependency was increased under Augustine's teaching that all humans are fallen, having corrupt hearts and minds. People who thought this way about themselves were more likely to conclude that they needed someone else, like the Church leadership, to tell them what is true.

Augustine's understanding of faith—to accept what the Church teaches—became the standard understanding across Europe throughout the Early Middle Ages. In accordance with this, the vast majority of people in Europe considered themselves Christian from the 6th to the 13th centuries.

During the Late Middle Ages (1250–1500), some aspects of Augustine's theology were overshadowed by the theology of Thomas Aquinas (1225–1274). The most significant change for our study is how Aquinas taught that the heart of man is fallen (corrupt and prone to sin), while the intellect of man is not fallen (not corrupt or prone to sin). People who followed Aquinas' teaching concluded their intellect is not fallen and so they began trusting their intellect to find truth. Aquinas' teaching that the human intellect was not fallen helped launch the Scientific Revolution of the 16th and 17th centuries.

Point 1.7: Shifting into the Scientific Revolution

Historians usually mark the start of the Scientific Revolution at the publication of Nicolaus Copernicus' book (1543) that showed the sun as the center of the solar system, rather than the earth. Then came Francis Bacon (1561–1626), Galileo (1564–1642), and Isaac Newton (1647–1727). These leaders, often called the "fathers of the Scientific Revolution,"[3] were believers in God, however, their thinking challenged the worldview of their time.

3 Johannes Kepler (1571–1630) is sometimes added to the list of fathers of the Scientific Revolution.

FATHERS OF THE SCIENTIFIC REVOLUTION:

| Copernicus | Bacon | Galileo | Newton |

Rather than seeing God as in control of all things, the Revolution led scientists to conclude that the world runs according to natural laws. Hence, the natural world could be studied and known.

Once this worldview was embraced by influential thinkers, they were free to apply their reasoning abilities to understand the physical world. No longer were their studies in astronomy undermined by thoughts that the stars are moved about by angelic beings. As soon as they concluded that the human body functions according to predictable laws, rather than the dictates of demons, studies in medicine flourished. This revolutionary thinking launched scientific discovery, which in turn, advanced almost every area of life.

Point 1.8: The Scientific Method Used to Discover Truth

The early scientists typically recognized two sources of truth: the Church as the source of truth about God and science as the source of truth about the natural world.

Scientific Revolution:
The Church as the Source of Truth about God;
Science as the Source of Truth about the Natural World

Systematic studies of the natural world became known as the "scientific method." The scientific method consisted of careful observations, measurements, and experimenting, accompanied by the formulation of hypotheses.

The *Oxford Living Dictionary* defines a hypothesis as "a proposed explanation made on the basis of limited evidence as a starting point for further investigation." Those who employed the scientific method would propose an explanation (a hypothesis) for some phenomenon they were observing and then continue testing to see if the hypothesis could accurately predict what would happen with future testing. The more accurately the hypothesis predicted future phenomena, the more certain scientists could trust the hypothesis.

In simple terms, repeated testing can reveal truth.

The scientific method became accepted as a philosophically approved method of discovering truth.

Point 1.9: The Separation of Faith and Knowledge

The early scientists did not reject God or the spiritual world. They simply concluded things in the natural world could be observed and tested, while things in the spiritual world were not subject to the scientific method. In time, the spiritual realm where God dwells became accepted as the "realm of faith" and the natural world became accepted as the "realm of science."

CHANGE IN THOUGHT
DURING THE SCIENTIFIC REVOLUTION:

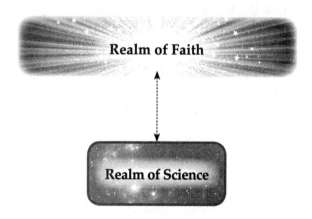

Next, those in positions of influence concluded that truths about the spiritual world can never be tested and, therefore, never be known with certainty. Hence, ideas about the spiritual world were thought of as "unknowable." In contrast, truths about the natural world were seen as subject to the scientific method and, therefore, "knowable."

This pitted faith against knowledge and led people to think of faith as the opposite of knowledge and reason. As a consequence, faith became less respectable intellectually. If we admit there is no proof for ideas associated with God and the spiritual world, we are admitting we really cannot be sure if they are true. As this perspective developed further, faith became understood as *the acceptance of ideas without any evidence* (In points 4.3-4.10, we will explain why this understanding is wrong and how true faith is built on evidence.)

Point 1.10: The Ever-Increasing Separation

The further along the Scientific Revolution advanced, the more the spiritual world decreased in significance while the natural world increased. Also, the separation between the spiritual and natural worlds became greater and greater in the minds of the people educated in the Western world.

INCREASING SEPARATION BETWEEN SPIRITUAL & NATURAL WORLDS

We should be grateful for the many advances science has given to humanity, but notice how Plato's separation of the spiritual world from the natural world was still fixed at the foundation of Western thought. As knowledge increased, philosophers and scientists built on Plato's dualistic cosmology, which continues to lie at the foundation of Western thought today.

Point 1.11: The Age of Enlightenment and Deism

Church leaders dominated Western philosophy throughout the Middle Ages and into the start of the Scientific Revolution. Then in the 18th century, a period known as the "Enlightenment" emerged, a period during which influential leaders rejected traditional religious, social, and political values. Instead, they saw themselves as replacing those traditional values with "rationalism," the belief that truth can only be derived from rational thought, which included the scientific method.

During the Enlightenment, many leaders switched their understanding of God to "deism." God was seen as having no involvement with the world, except in the fact that he started it, and after the world ends, will judge it. With deism, the world is often portrayed as a watch and God as the Great Watchmaker; he made the watch, and then stepped back to let the watch run on its own.

Deism was a clear departure from the traditional Christian understanding, that God is very involved with the daily activities of humanity and in governing the natural world. Deism resulted in moving God far away from the daily affairs of life. Since God was removed, deists could no longer envision God working any miracles in this world. Nor could deists accept the concept of God coming into this world in Jesus. For a loyal deist, Jesus may be a great teacher but never worked miracles or rose from the dead.

Progression of Thought Leading to Atheism/Agnosticism

Intellectuals such as Voltaire (in France), Thomas Jefferson, and Benjamin Franklin (in the USA) were strong proponents of deism. At the founding of the United States, there was such a mixture of deists and traditional Christians, that historians today debate whether there were more deists or Christians among the founding fathers.

During the same period, leaders antagonistic to the Church rose to the forefront to further develop the philosophical progression. Secular professors at universities in Europe became especially forceful in diminishing the influence of the Church. Atheistic professors worked hard at convincing students that anything once valued as evidence for faith was foolishness. The Church and the Bible were constant targets under attack. Professors proposed many progressions of thought that led students to conclude faith is an item of disdain to be discarded by the intellectually enlightened.

Point 1.12: Natural Theology to the Rescue

While the Enlightenment thinkers were promoting science united with logic as the only path to discover truth, some God-fearing philosophers wrestled to restore the intellectual credibility of faith. Since many had concluded the unknowable, spiritual world offers no reliable truth about God, they thought perhaps they could look into the natural world to see evidence of God in the spiritual world. The related studies became known as "natural theology."[4]

The label, "natural theology," was meant to contrast with "revealed theology" which referred to developing thoughts

---

4 Some leaders, such as Thomas Aquinas, had worked in natural theology much earlier than the Enlightenment, but here we are focusing on the role natural theology played as a major movement within the historical philosophical progression. In that context, natural theology was a movement to oppose the atheism of the Enlightenment.

about God starting with Scripture or religious experience. Philosophers during the Enlightenment were rejecting ideas originating with the Bible or religious experience, so natural theology was an attempt to show truths about God evident from nature alone.

Studies in natural theology corresponded to what Paul wrote in the Bible about creation revealing the invisible attributes of God:

> *For since the creation of the world His invisible attributes, His eternal power and divine nature, have been clearly seen, being understood through what has been made . . . .*

Romans 1:20

Philosophers promoting natural theology did not refer to these words of Paul to try to prove the existence of God. Rather, they offered arguments similar to Paul's argument that creation is evidence of God's existence and nature.

Point 1.13: Isolation of the Spiritual and Natural Worlds

Natural theology slowed the philosophical progression toward atheism but not for long.

Emmanuel Kant (1724–1804) wrote a book entitled, *Critique of Pure Reason*, in which he proposed a progression of thought that totally separated and isolated the spiritual/faith/unknowable/ religious world from the physical/provable/ knowable/scientific world. Rather than trying to convince people faith does have some evidential support, Kant argued that the world of faith does not need any evidence to support it. In fact, according to Kant, the spiritual world of

Kant

Progression of Thought Leading to Atheism/Agnosticism

God is so *transcendent,* we should not expect anything of the spiritual world to be subject to our communication or human logic.

EMMANUEL KANT:
TOTAL SEPARATION OF THE SPIRITUAL AND NATURAL WORLDS

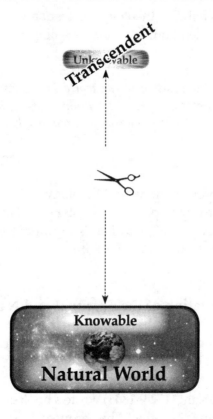

Kant's view of reality implied the spiritual and natural worlds are so different from one another, it would be impossible for the logic or words that function in one world to serve any purpose in the other world. Therefore, even if God wanted to communicate from his spiritual world to our world, he could not! No communication is possible, because God and his world are transcendent according to Kant. This means God has not communicated with humanity, God did not become human in

Jesus Christ, and the Bible does not reveal to us anything about God or the spiritual world.

Kant's ideas did not achieve what he desired. Rather than accepting the existence of a transcendent spiritual world, scholars accepted Kant's strict compartmentalizing of the spiritual world and the natural world. Atheists celebrated Kant's admittance that there is no evidence and never will be any evidence in the natural world of God's existence in the spiritual world.

Kant's cosmology, with two totally independent, isolated worlds, was accepted by all of the major universities in Europe by 1850. The famous biologist Stephen Gould (1941–2002) explained it well, teaching that faith and science should occupy separate "non-over-lapping magisteria."[5] Today, Kant's view is the basis of almost all modern secular philosophical thought and liberal theological thought.

Point 1.14: Kierkegaard's Leap into Foolishness

Kierkegaard

Then came Soren Kierkegaard (1813–1855), who proposed another way to gain knowledge about God. Soren built on Kant's view that the world of faith is totally separate and isolated from the natural world. However, Soren taught that people may gain evidence of God by surrendering all reason and taking a blind leap of faith into the arms of God.

By the late 19th century, most liberal theologians followed in Soren's path. They accepted Kant's teaching that there is no natural proof for the existence of God, but, as Soren taught, a person may experience God after a leap of faith.

5 Cited in Francis Collins. *The Language of God* (New York: Free Press. 2006), pt. 5.

SOREN KIERKEGAARD:
GOD MAY REVEAL HIMSELF TO THOSE WHO TAKE A LEAP OF FAITH

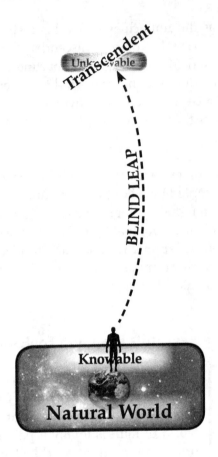

Point 1.15: It Is Settled—There Is No Evidence of God

It was not long until atheistic philosophers reinterpreted Soren's leap of faith as a leap into foolishness. They could accept that some people have a psychological or imagined experience when they take a blind leap, but that psychological or imagined experience was just being confused with God.

24

So Soren's leap had no effect toward convincing atheists that God exists in Kant's transcendent world. However, with Kant and Kierkegaard's help, most liberal theologians were now on the side of the atheists with the idea that there is no evidence in the natural world for the existence of God in the spiritual world. Western philosophers had succeeded in developing a progression of thought that led them to conclude:

There is no evidence of God's existence!

Nietzsche

The German philosopher Friedrich Nietzsche (1844–1900) declared, "God is dead!" With this statement, he was saying we humans have eliminated God from our own lives by developing rational ways to explain the world without God.

Some leaders in the world of academia were not satisfied to leave God and religion in the world of the unknowable. Some atheists felt compelled to destroy all residue of faith. They saw all religion and belief in God as superstition keeping society in darkness and bondage.

The famous evolutionist, Richard Dawkins (born 1941), ridiculed faith teaching that:

> Faith is the great cop-out, the great excuse to evade the need to think and evaluate evidence. Faith is belief in spite of, even perhaps because of, a lack of evidence. . . . Faith, being belief that isn't based on evidence, is the principle vice of any religion.[6]

Some atheistic scientists went so far as to totally eliminate the spiritual world from their worldview. The famous astronomer, Carl Sagan (1934–1996) proclaimed, "The cosmos is all there is or ever was or ever will be." For many philoso-

---

6 Cited in Francis Collins. *The Language of God* (New York: Free Press. 2006), pt. 4.

phers and scientists, the natural world emerged on the scene—
as if it alone exists.

CARL SAGAN:
"THE COSMOS IS ALL THERE IS OR EVER WAS OR EVER WILL BE"

By the late 19th century, atheistic philosophers felt they
had turned a corner in the advancement of civilization. They
celebrated because they "had gotten rid of God."

Point 1.16: Finally, God Is Dead!

We have now summarized the 2,400-year progression of
philosophical thought concerning the subject of God's existence.
Key features are:

1. The foundation of Plato's dualistic cosmology

2. The increasing separation of the spiritual and natural worlds

3. The association of faith with the spiritual world and the
   scientific method with the natural world

4. Contrasting faith with knowledge, then defining faith as
   the acceptance of ideas without evidence

5. Labeling of the spiritual world as transcendent or even
   non-existent, meaning nothing can be known about the
   spiritual world and, if God exists, he is totally unreachable

6. Concluding there is no evidence for God's existence

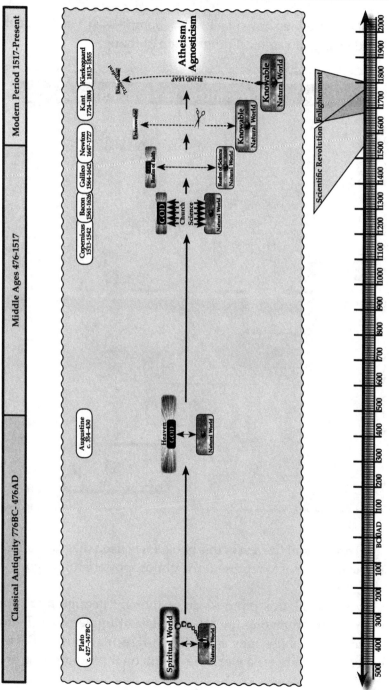

Progression of Thought Leading to Atheism/Agnosticism

The timeline shown below is a compressed version of the 2,400 year philosophical progression of thought.

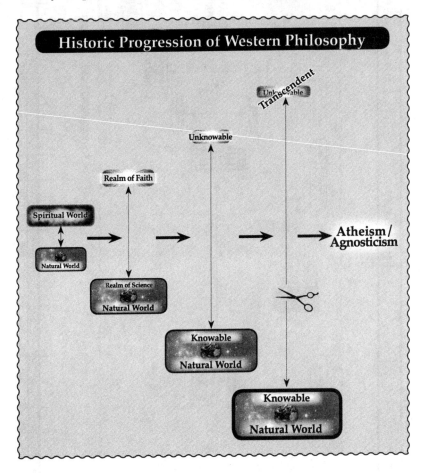

Throughout the rest of this book, I will use a diagram similar to the one above to represent the philosophical progression.

After 1850, this progression of thought became more and more common among the intelligentsia at universities. Today, professors of philosophy and religion at secular universities are expected to embrace a worldview built on this progression and they would be unlikely to continue holding their position if they strayed too far. To various degrees, instructors in other fields of study are also expected to hold this fundamental worldview with Plato's dualistic cosmology at the foundation and Kant's moving of the spiritual world beyond the reach of communication and reason.

This has become the most common atheistic/agnostic way of thinking in the modern educated world.

Point 1.17: The Front Door of Atheism

At the end of the philosophical journey, the student of philosophy is *ushered to the front door of atheism/agnosticism*. To understand this, we must consider atheism and agnosticism separately. First, let's deal with atheism.

Western philosophy only leads to the front door of atheism because the philosophical progression *does not prove* atheism.

It is logically impossible to prove atheism because it is impossible to prove a negative. Someone may say, "God is not in my world!", but that does not prove God is not in someone else's world, or in a different galaxy, or in a different dimension. It is impossible to look everywhere.

Another reason followers of Western philosophy cannot prove God's non-existence is because Western philosophy concluded nothing can be known about the spiritual world. That works both ways. If it is impossible to know anything about the spiritual world, then it is impossible to know if God exists or doesn't exist in the spiritual world. This is another reason Western philosophy cannot logically conclude there is no God.

Progression of Thought Leading to Atheism/Agnosticism

When people first hear this truth they are often surprised. Atheists typically portray themselves as the rational ones who would never accept any idea without evidence. That portrayal is so convincing, people often accept it as fact. In reality, there is no evidence for the non-existence of God.

For this reason, the Western philosophical progression ushers the student to the front door of atheism, but *an individual must take a blind leap to go through the door.* Since no one can prove God's non-existence, atheism is always a choice not supported by logic.

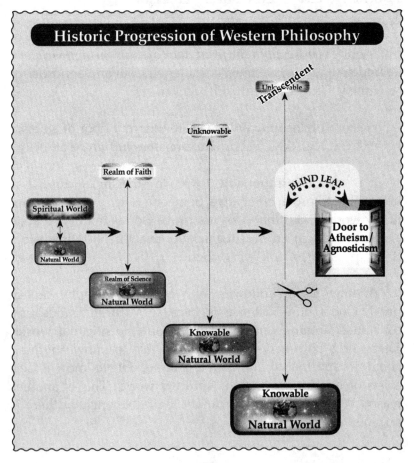

Point 1.18: Reasons to Become an Atheist

Although there is *no proof* of God's non-existence, individuals may have *reasons* why they embrace atheism. For example, some atheists will say they cannot conceive of God existing when there is so much evil in the world. Others say they became an atheist because they learned about the horrific acts of violence committed by religious people in history. And others may become atheists because they don't like obnoxious religious people, but do admire certain atheists. Indeed, these may be *reasons* for a person to become an atheist, but none of these prove God does not exist.

Many people become atheists while submerged in higher education, because there is pressure to take the step. Students who believe in God are sometimes ridiculed, even publicly in classrooms. They are made to feel archaic, still clinging to the superstitions of the Middle Ages, before the Enlightenment.

Such pressures extend beyond the universities, sometimes passing down through teachers and administrators who lead at high and junior high schools. Presently, some teenagers and young adults embrace atheism / agnosticism because it is the vogue thing to do. Many young people embrace atheism / agnosticism for at least a time, to try it on for size.

Point 1.19: The Front Door of Agnosticism

Knowing atheism cannot be supported rationally, some people choose *agnosticism*.

The most widely held type of agnosticism is also irrational, but as I explain why, I need to carefully define what I mean by agnosticism. Here I am using the definition that corresponds with the historic progression of philosophical thought, so we can refer to this as "philosophical agnosticism." A philosophical agnostic is "a person who believes that nothing is known or can be known of the existence or nature of God" (taken from the *Oxford English Dictionary*).

In order to see why philosophical agnosticism—as defined here—is not supported by logical thought, notice how philosophical agnosticism does not say whether or not God exists, but only that *no one knows if God exists.*

That leaves open the possibility that God does exist.

WITH PHILOSOPHICAL AGNOSTICISM GOD MAY EXIST

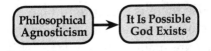

If God does exist, then there are two possibilities in the ongoing progression of thought: either God has not revealed himself or he has revealed himself.

If God has not revealed himself, then no one knows if God exists. On the other hand, if God has revealed himself, then the person to whom he has revealed himself does know God exists.

TWO POSSIBILITIES IF GOD EXISTS

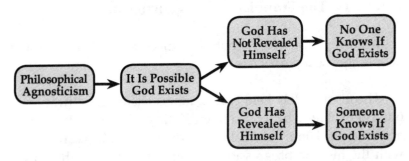

Both of these progressions of thought are logical possibilities. Yet, philosophical agnosticism denies the second possibility.

In pointing this out, I am not saying God has revealed himself. I am simply saying it is logically possible. I am not proposing any certain person to whom God has revealed himself. I am simply saying it is possible he has revealed himself to someone in the world or even to many people. Furthermore, it is not possible for us to talk to every human being on earth who has ever lived or lives today. It is impossible for us to prove God has not revealed himself to someone.

When agnostics say no one knows if God exists, they are assuming God has not revealed himself to anyone. That is an assumption that was fixed in Western philosophy when philosophers labeled the spiritual world "transcendent." But it is pure assumption to say the spiritual world is transcendent in the sense of God not revealing himself.

PHILOSOPHICAL AGNOSTICISM IS BUILT ON THE ASSUMPTION THAT GOD DOES NOT REVEAL HIMSELF

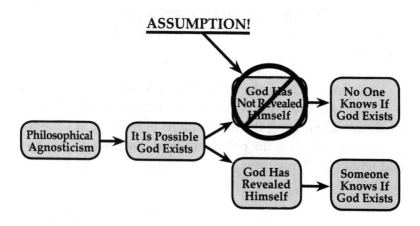

A progression of thought built on such a key assumption is logically indefensible.

Progression of Thought Leading to Atheism/Agnosticism

Point 1.20: Intellectually Integrous Agnosticism

For agnostics to hold a logical position they must abandon philosophical agnosticism and embrace common agnosticism which simply says, *"I don't know if God exists."* This position can be held with intellectual integrity.

However, it is more difficult to hold to common agnosticism because it leaves the individual responsible to God if he exists.

This is in contrast to philosophical agnosticism because that view says it is impossible to know if God exists. If it is impossible to know, then the individual is not responsible to know if God exists. If God has not revealed himself, it would be unjust for God to hold the individual responsible to live as if he does exist. In other words, the person who says no one knows if God exists has absolved himself from the responsibility to live as if God exists.

On the other hand, if I don't know if God exists, it may be my responsibility to find out. Furthermore, if God has revealed himself to me in any way, and I am denying or ignoring it, then it would be just for God to hold me accountable to live as if he does exist.

I am not touching the subject as to what it means to live as if God exists. That is a subject for another book. Here we are simply identifying the implications of holding to common agnosticism which is the only form of agnosticism that can be held with logical integrity.

Summary of Section One

The historic Western philosophical progression ushers people to the front door of atheism / agnosticism. It presents a specific progression of thought, like rolling out a red carpet upon which people can walk. That red carpet ends at the door of decision.

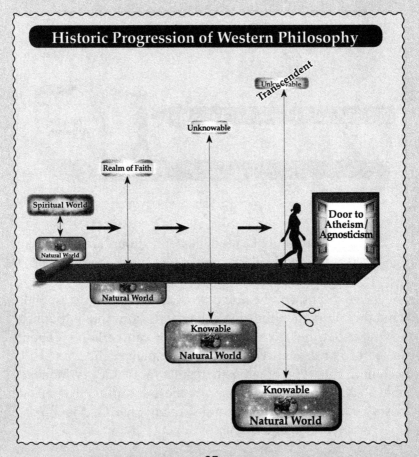

Historic Progression of Western Philosophy

Transcendent
Unknowable
Unknowable
Realm of Faith
Spiritual World
Natural World
Natural World
Knowable Natural World
Knowable Natural World
Door to Atheism / Agnosticism

Progression of Thought Leading to Atheism/Agnosticism

The progression of thought that is taught in a typical philosophy classroom is comparable to the progression of thought laid out by an evangelist in a church meeting. At the end of the evangelist's presentation, the attentive listener is standing face to face with a decision. So also, students of philosophy eventually find themselves standing at the doorway of decision.

If students of philosophy step through the doorway into atheism, they will be taking a blind leap because there is no known progression of thought that logically leads to atheism.

EMBRACING ATHEISM ALWAYS REQUIRES A BLIND LEAP

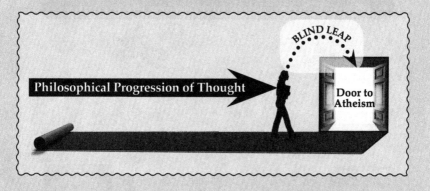

On the other hand, if a student steps through the door into agnosticism they will fall into one of two types of agnosticism.

As we discussed, the first type of agnosticism corresponds with the Western philosophical progression and is defined as "the belief that nothing is known or can be known about the nature or existence of God." As explained in point 1.19, becoming this type of agnostic results in a logically indefensible position because it is based on the assumption that if God exists he has not revealed himself to anyone. That is impossible for anyone to determine.

Embracing Philosophical Agnosticism Always Results in a Logically Indefensible Position

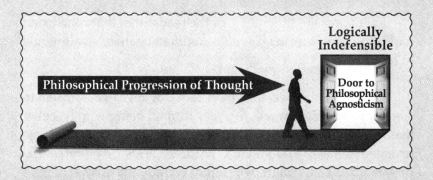

Individuals who step through the door into the second type of agnosticism (common agnosticism) will say, "*I don't know if God exists.*" Taking that step leaves the person in a blind position, not knowing if God exists and still responsible to him if he does exist.

Embracing Common Agnosticism Leaves One in a Blind Position

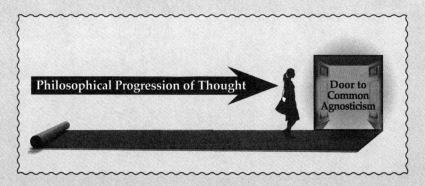

There is one more significant conclusion that should have become evident here in Section 1. It is a partial answer to the question which is the title of this book: *Has God Proven His Existence?* We have not yet answered this question completely, but at this point, we can conclude that it is logically incorrect to say that God has not proven his existence.

It may present difficulties for the reader that that conclusion had to be communicated with a double negative, so allow me to rephrase it.

No one can prove that God has not revealed himself to someone. No one can talk to every human being who has ever lived or is now living. Therefore, no one knows if God has revealed himself to someone. So then, *"Has God Proven His Existence?"* At this point, we cannot confidently answer, "Yes." But we can confidently say it is logically incorrect to answer, "No."

SECTION TWO

The Values of Atheism/Agnosticism

Anyone who follows and embraces the historic Western philosophical progression of thought and steps through the door into atheism /agnosticism will discover a set of values that corresponds to atheism /agnosticism. Of course, there are some possible minor variations but arriving at the most fundamental values logically following from atheism /agnosticism is as inevitable as $2 + 2 = 4$.

Understanding those fundamental values will help you understand what is going on in the world around you and why the world has changed so dramatically in recent years. More importantly, you will be able to see if those values have become your own. You will know where those thoughts originated and if they justify your continued loyalty.

Point 2.1: Under the Influence of Western Philosophy

Everyone in the Western world is influenced to some degree by the thoughts of Western philosophy.

However, it is the university student sitting in a philosophically-influenced classroom that has to face the full impact of philosophical thought. Each student will see if their own traditional, cultural, and family values can withstand the onslaught of the accumulated reasoning of the brilliant philosophers. Before the process is complete, each student of philosophy will stand before the door of atheism / agnosticism and have to decide whether to step inside.

The student must stand at the threshold alone, having to decide for themselves whether to step across that threshold. No one can make that step for them. Fellow students may offer advice, but the decision must be made independently.

THE STEP INTO ATHEISM / AGNOSTICISM IS MADE ALONE

Students who resist stepping through the doorway will only do so by fighting off some ridicule and accusations of being unenlightened and afraid of facing reality. They may also deal with the threat of being ostracized by the more militant ones who have already stepped inside.

Students who step into atheism / agnosticism will enter into a new home—a home without God.

Once a person enters that home they will find a community in which every person shares similar values. The initiate is sure to find new friends who can offer an affirming smile or nod. They are the intelligent ones who have become like their favorite professors and authors, the smartest people in the room. They see themselves as enlightened, and therefore, on the forefront of cultural and intellectual evolution. They are the bravest ones who have embraced reality, the reality that people are alone in this world with no God to hold their hand.

Point 2.2: Nothing Is Sacred

Those who embrace the historic philosophic progression will conclude that the spiritual world and God are transcendent or non-existent. Hence, nothing can be known about the spiritual world or God. If nothing can be known, then the spiritual world and God are irrelevant or even non-existent.

In philosophical thought, "transcendent" means totally beyond, separated, and unreachable. So if the spiritual world is transcendent, we live a world void of the spirit. Everything in our world is physical.

This means humans are physical beings. We came into existence through natural processes. Nothing spiritual was ever added to the mix. People have no soul. There is no afterlife. What you see is what you are.

If God is non-existent or transcendent, then nothing can derive its meaning from him. This concept becomes clearer when we contrast it with a statement in the USA's *Declaration of Independence:*

> We hold these truths to be self-evident, that all men are created equal, that they are endowed by their creator with certain unalienable Rights, that among these are Life, Liberty and the pursuit of Happiness.

This statement is false according to the Western philosophical progression. If God is non-existent or transcendent, then people are *not* endowed by their creator with any rights.

Since rights do not come from God in a world where God is transcendent or does not exist, we need to determine if there is any foundation for the rights of the individual. The best Western philosophy has been able to offer is that the rights of any individual are those which are assigned to them by society.

Therefore, children only have value if society chooses to value them. With the mother of the child being most involved and responsible, the mother is most significant in assigning value to the child, including the right to life. When the elderly are of no benefit to society, it would be perfectly reasonable to discard them. Also, because life has no inherent or God-given value, suicide is reasonable and permissible.

If indeed, the spiritual world is transcendent or non-existent, then nothing is sacred. By sacred, we mean "deserving of reverence because of a connection to God." If God is transcendent, nothing in the physical world has any connection to him.

If nothing is sacred, then human life is not sacred. Then

what humans do is not sacred. Sexual intimacy is not sacred. Marriage is not sacred. Commitments are not sacred. Love is not sacred.[7] If there is no spiritual world, then nothing is sacred.

Point 2.3: The Place of Religion in the Modern World

When religion (at least the monotheistic religions) is doing what it claims to do, it serves a purpose, primarily being to guide and encourage people to relate properly to God.

That purpose makes no sense to those who follow Western philosophy into atheism. Since atheists do not believe God exists, they lose the understanding that religion could ever possibly serve such a purpose. Instead, they see religious leaders as making up information about God. Hence, those religious leaders are deluded themselves or charlatans deceiving the masses.

Some atheists /agnostics will still recognize a small benefit to religion, primarily being an aid for weak-minded people to make sense out of life. Religion may give people a reference point to organize their worldview and, hence, deal with life, death, and suffering in this world. Atheists /agnostics may also recognize a benefit in that religion creates culture, traditions, and rituals around which people may form communities. Seeing these benefits, some atheists /agnostics see wisdom in allowing religion to continue within society.

However, atheists /agnostics who allow religion to continue want the world governed with the awareness that no one knows if any one religion is right or wrong. Therefore, all religions are equal—equally unprovable. If Christianity is allowed, Islam

---

7 Some atheists /agnostics still recognize something sacred about love. However, they cannot explain it, and their understanding of sacred has nothing to do with a connection to God.

should be allowed. Buddhism, Judaism, and Hinduism should be allowed. It does not matter. If one religion is tolerated, all religions should be tolerated.

According to most atheists / agnostics, the main problem is not religion, but the religious nut who thinks his religion is more right than the religion of others. So if we allow religion to continue in society we still do not have to tolerate religious fanatics who are trying to destroy or convert all who are of a different religion. So long as no one takes their religion too seriously, all religions will be able to coexist.

In the mind of the atheist, civilization will gradually mature. Then all religions will fade out of existence. But during the present premature state of civilization, we should give the unenlightened masses the religious crutches they need, but eventually, everyone will mature to the point where God is not needed any more than Santa Claus is needed.

Point 2.4: No God, No Absolutes

We have stated the primary purpose of the monotheistic religions to guide and encourage people to relate properly to God. Atheists / agnostics have no framework to understand that purpose or function since they see God as non-existent or at least transcendent with no connection to this world.

Since atheists / agnostics recognize no connection between religious leaders and God, atheists / agnostics see no reason religious leaders have any authority to tell humanity what God desires. Before the Enlightenment, religious leaders had authority because they supposedly had some connection with God, either through contact with him or through the study of religious books that revealed God's will. After God lost his access to the natural world—at least, that is what seemed to happen—religious leaders lost their authority. With no authority, religious leaders became noisy gongs, clanging away annoying sounds that the enlightened did not want to hear. Especially annoying have been the religious leaders who try to tell others how to act.

But rejoice! Atheists/agnostics are announcing to all that we can be free of the dictates of religion. There is no God demanding sacrifice or service. He never did want our money or obedience.

Furthermore, since there is no God, there are no absolutes for right and wrong. Without God, there is no standard. Sin is obsolete. Religion is bondage. Guilt is culturally induced and should be overcome. Freedom is the cry! Since the Enlightenment, atheistic/agnostic leaders have been celebrating that freedom and announcing the good news to all willing to listen.

In this new world, sexual freedom is one sign—the most prominent sign—of a liberated lifestyle. The person who can engage in sexual acts that were previously considered illicit has stepped into modernity. Enlightened people are expected to express their approval of others who have thrown off traditional sexual prohibitions. Better yet, they express disdain for religiously uptight prudes who try to impose their sexual restrictions upon others.

Point 2.5: The Package of Philosophical Values

The progression of Western philosophy leads to the set of values that we have been discussing. Those values are a package. They come together because they are all logically consistent and connected.

The Step into Atheism /Agnosticism Is a Step into a Specific Set of Values

All Is Physical

Rights & Values Are Assigned by Society, Not Derived from God

Abortion, Euthanasia, & Suicide Are Perfectly Justified

Life, Love, Sex, Marriage, & Commitments Are Not Sacred

Nothing Is Sacred

Religion Only Serves a Purpose for the Weak-minded

All Religions Are Equal & Irrational

No Religious Fanaticism Should be Tolerated

Religion Is Temporary

Religious Leaders Have No Authority to Dictate Right from Wrong

There Are No Absolutes

Sin & Guilt Are Obsolete

True Freedom Is Freedom from Religion

True Freedom Is Marked by Sexual Freedom

The masses in Western society have not embraced the whole philosophical package. Most have two sets of thoughts battling for supremacy in their mind: traditional thoughts built on the existence of God and modern philosophical thoughts built on the non-existence or transcendence of God.

Most Westerners do not know from where their atheistic / agnostic-based thoughts originated. They do not connect their thoughts about faith lacking evidence back to the university professor who explained to his students how the Scientific Revolution separated faith from reason. They never connect their disinterest in sacred things to Kant's proclamation that the spiritual world is transcendent. Nor do they connect their lax attitudes about sexual promiscuity to the rejection of religious authority during the Enlightenment.

The thoughts and values of Western philosophy trickle down and out to the masses like seeds dispersed by the wind. Those seeds of thought lodge into every crevice of the mind, with some seeds eventually taking root.

Point 2.6: The 1960s as a Product of Western Philosophy

From time to time, the seed thoughts of Western philosophy grow and mature into a harvest visible to the whole world. One such time was during the cultural revolution of the 1960s. Students at prominent universities could no longer keep silent. The ideas of Western philosophy had been dangled before classrooms of students for more than a generation. The fullness of times arrived and a revolution burst into the open within Western civilization.

Music played a central role, with an eruption of new bands traveling the world. That music was so original and different it created a clear demarcation between the younger hip generation and the older generation who could not understand or enjoy the new sounds. Those music groups sang about free love and drug experimentation, along with other subjects previously taboo in open public settings.

Many of the young people were naive and simply swept into the revolution by the shared music and excitement. But there were others acting as prophets speaking philosophical change into the wind through songs, poems, cliches, books, and discussions. As Simon and Garfunkel sang, "The words of the prophets are written on the subway walls."

The seeded thoughts that changed society sprouted as catchphrases that anyone could remember and repeat. Timothy Leary (1920–1996), once a professor at Harvard University, coined the famous phrases, "Think for yourself and question authority," and "Turn on, tune in, drop out."

During the late 1960s, the media talked incessantly about "the generation gap," referring to a supposedly impassable chasm separating those over 30 from those under 30 years of age. (Somehow hip university professors always fit into the under 30 crowd). The media's use of the terminology "generation gap" was presented as reporting the facts, but the more it was reported, the more it became fact. Young people concluded they could not talk to their parents who were too old and bound to traditions to understand. In the meantime, parents over 30 accepted the existence of a generation gap believing it was hopeless to even try to talk to or influence their teenage and young adult children.

Once the gap was widely accepted as fact, the younger generation saw themselves as detached from and somewhat ahead of their parents in cultural and intellectual ways. As a result, young adults questioned the values of previous generations, seeing traditional values as especially repugnant. Then it was natural for them to embrace political, religious, and social values directly in conflict with their parents' generation. Hence, they were more receptive to the philosophical values being offered as attractive, modern alternatives.

Another seed-thought that took on momentum during the 1960s was, "No one can legislate morality." There was enough truth in this to find root in the minds of many because people associated morality in general with sexual morality and then reasoned that people will always find ways to satisfy their sexual drives no matter what laws are placed upon them. However, the idea that no one can legislate morality carried with it several negative implications, including the idea that sexual passion is so powerful no one can control themselves, so we are all victims who would be better off yielding to the related passions.

Ideas corresponding to Western philosophy also filtered into child rearing during the 1960s. Dr. Benjamin Spock's (1903–1998) writings were the most popular on the subject. Some of his teachings brought harm, but some also benefited society including his admonitions for parents to be less rigid, show more affection, and treat each child as an individual.

At the same time, young parents embraced a new value to not teach their children any religion so they could "grow up and make up their own mind." This cliché fit well with the emerging philosophical values that children should be allowed to think for themselves and not forced to follow the beliefs of their parents. It also corresponded with the philosophical ideas that all religions are equal and unimportant. It resulted in a generation detached from many of the traditional Christian values once embraced by Western society.

Point 2.7: Needing a North Star to Structure Daily Life

Since the values of Western philosophy erupted on the open stage in the 1960s, the world has shifted. The repercussions persist today. In particular, the masses are looking for a new foundation upon which to build their lives.

If God is transcendent or non-existent, no one can look

to him for instructions on how to live. Nor can they look to religious leaders who pretend to know what God wants people to do. For followers of the Western philosophical progression, traditional standards for human behavior have vanished.

Yet, people get up every morning asking, "What should I do today?" They want instructions. At the very least, they *need* an overriding mission around which they can structure their day.

Philosophers, thinkers, political leaders, writers, singers, and teachers have attempted to come up with some overriding mission for all of humanity. Western philosophers have been searching for this for hundreds of years. It has been the pursuit of the secular masses since the 1960s. They have attempted to find some north star which defines their reason for living.

Prominent among those answers is the modern environmental movement. Some may replace God for Mother Earth, while theists may say God gave us responsibility to steward this earth. Once life is anchored in either north star the individual can slide into a daily routine of riding a bicycle, planting a garden, shopping at the health food store, and recycling as much as possible. Of course, people do not like to think their daily routines are being directed, but give any person one north star and their daily routine will soon fall into alignment.

Other north stars have been proposed such as making the world a better place. Some have chosen social justice or to defend the rights of the oppressed. Many have oriented their life toward creating a perfect society where all people are treated equally, with equal access to finances, education, and medical services.

Another north star for many is the threat of global warming and climate change. Whether or not the masses believe it is a real threat, it offers a purpose greater than any of us. If science brings us an answer to solve this threat, humans in their need for a mission will find some other world-encompassing challenge that requires the attention, energy, and focus of the masses. Without God, such a threat provides a purpose for daily life.

Another north star is built on nihilism which we will define in a moment (point 2.10). For now, we can say that the progressive philosophical path leads to a life with no meaning. Therefore, adherents claim each person must create their own meaning. Some create their own meaning by simply enjoying life, eating, drinking, and being merry for tomorrow we die. In other words, doing what makes themselves happy is their highest aim.

Most modern Westerners have a hodgepodge of these and other values governing their daily decisions. Some are the values of their foreparents from before the 1960s, values such as working hard, paying bills, quietly enduring hardship, staying married, striving to give their children an advantage, and serving one's country. Some modern Westerners are more strongly a product of their parents who reached adulthood during the 1960s, and hence, they mistrust authority, are concerned for civil rights, disdain polluters of the environment, reject war, and resent laws that infringe on personal freedom. Others continue thinking about the behavior desired by the God in whom they believe. Most people in the Western world have a whole mixture of all these and other values, but the Western philosophical values find their way into the mix.

It is the people who have focused on only one set of values whom we consider radicals, whether those values are built on the environmental movement, improving the world, social justice, global warming, or wanting to do what their God desires.

Point 2.8: Governed by Subjective Morality

It is worth mentioning one more standard for living that atheists have been talking about in recent years. Rather than looking for a mission bigger and outside of oneself, many atheists talk about "subjective morality." By looking within, people are trusted to come up with their own set of moral standards. Atheists promoting this way of determining right from wrong talk about simply "being good" without God or religion.[8]

This perspective of atheists is built on a very positive view of human nature, that people will be good if left alone to govern themselves.

From the perspective of Evangelical Christianity, moral subjectivity is naive. Evangelicals are ever aware of the fall of humanity (the concept that all of humanity is corrupt and prone to evil because of the sin of Adam and Eve) and also the historical evidence of people, including atheistic societies— especially atheistic societies—committing atrocities toward each other.[9]

A good example that reveals the divergent views of atheists versus Christians pertaining to this subject is to consider the Christian's question sometimes addressed to atheists, "Since you have no absolutes, why don't you atheists go out, and rape and steal all you want?" The atheists calmly answer, "We

---

8 "Situational ethics" also came into many discussions about determining right from wrong, but it was promoted primarily by liberal theologians. Situational ethics takes into account the particular context of an act, rather than judging it according to absolute moral standards, such as those written in the Bible. Most adherents identified unconditional love as the highest end.

9 There have been many wars fought for religious ideals, but atheistic societies have committed the greatest atrocities: Stalin being responsible for more than 20 million deaths, Mao Zedong's regime for approximately 70 million, etc. All total, atheistic societies have slaughtered more than one million people per year averaged over the twentieth century.

do." You may have to think for a moment about that answer to understand what atheists are saying. Their answer is meant to shock the one asking the question. After the shock has had its effect, they may add, "We are raping and stealing all we want but the good news is that we don't want to—so we don't do it."

With this statement, atheists drive home their belief that they are not bad people who want to rape and steal. Furthermore, atheists can reinforce their belief that they don't need religion to tell them what is right and wrong. Instead, atheists promoting subjective reality believe most people will act right out of their own nature, which they believe is inherently oriented toward doing right.

Subjective morality is one more governing principle that has been proposed for people without God. In reality, this and all governing principles are passing vapors with no substance. As the famous Russian novelist, Fyodor Dostoevsky, pointed out, "If God is dead, then everything is permitted."[10] There is no right and wrong if there is no God.

Point 2.9: You Are Dead

If there is no right and wrong, there are no good or evil people. Everyone is equal in the sense of moral value.

Besides, you are probably a collection of chemicals, organized by random mutations, then selected and accumulated over the course of millions of years. Everything you do is a product of nature or nurture. There is never a time you act as a truly independent agent. You have no free will. No personhood. You are just actions and reactions, a machine, a robot destined to rust and rot away. There is no real you. There never is a you.

---

10 Dostoevsky (1821–1881) was an Orthodox Christian.

And when you die, the game is over. When you die, you will leave nothing behind. You will be forgotten. You are just dust, and to dust, you will return.

You will cease to exist, and that is all you will do—cease to exist, rather than die—because you never were alive, at least, not in the sense previous generations understood. Since chemicals are dead, you have always been dead.

When you cease to exist, all your thoughts will cease. But then, your thoughts never did account for anything anyway. They were simply electrical impulses traveling down neural pathways.

So also, the people around you are just a collection of chemicals arranged in complex patterns. They too are robots not really alive.

In a world of robots, love is an illusion. It is foolish to love a machine that is just made of chemicals. Two robots bumping into each other. Sexual relationships are just "hookups," purely physical connections with nothing meaningful produced. For adherents, there is no such thing as a lasting connection. Love is nothing more than a flow of certain chemicals through the bloodstream. Love is empty. Love is nothing.[11]

Point 2.10: The End of Western Philosophy Is Nihilism

Even if there were good people, bad things would happen to them just like it happens to bad people. If there is no God, then there is no force holding bad things away from good people. Anything can happen to anyone.

---

11 Some atheists / agnostics recognize some metaphysical value in love, but they do not attempt to explain it.

The Values of Atheism /Agnosticism

It does not matter anyway because the earth may be blown away tomorrow and no one would exist to remember it. Nothing has meaning or makes sense. Life is absurd. Life is a joke. This is reality. [12]

When someone comes to this awareness, they have arrived at truth and maturity according to the predominant Western philosophical progression. Life has no meaning. All is absurd. That awareness is called "nihilism,"[13] which means "nothingness."

WESTERN PHILOSOPHICAL PROGRESSION LEADS TO NIHILISM

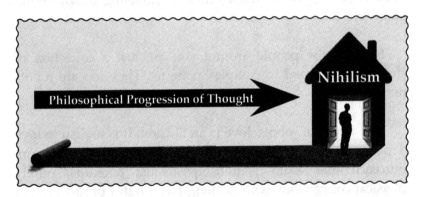

This is part of the atheistic/agnostic package. If you step across the threshold into atheism, you will be set free from God and his rules but you will also lose all meaning to your existence. If there is no God, there is no you. Welcome to nihilism.

---

12 Being told this can be especially disturbing to people previously trained in Christian thought because Christians are taught that God is with them and God has a plan for their life. Depending upon what stream of Christianity a person has been a part of, they will also in various degrees have a concept of God as a loving father. It is from that loving father that the individual's purpose is thought to have originated. It is personal, intimate, and life-forming. When a Christian, who is trained in the awareness of a father-given purpose, is told there is no God, the results can be disillusioning, even devastating. All sense of a God-given identity and purpose vanishes.

13 Philosophers define several different forms of nihilism. Here we are using the word in a general sense.

Point 2.11: Existentialism as the Answer to Despair

Modern atheistic philosophers readily admit their philosophical progression of thought leads *all followers to despair.* They talk about an individual stepping into an "existential attitude," when they experience a complete sense of disorientation, confusion, and dread in the face of realizing life is meaningless and absurd.

It is difficult to understand many artistic masterpieces of the early 20th century, without also understanding the philosophical topics of the period.[14]

The Scream by Edvard Munch

The best solution to nihilism that Western atheistic philosophers have come up with is the decision for each and every person to find or create their own meaning. Philosophers call it "existentialism." Since life has no meaning, each person must create their own existence.

Compare this to the analogous conclusion that human life is not sacred (point 2.2). Since there is no God, people have no God-given value. The only value anyone has is that which is assigned to them by society, and a baby has no value unless the mother assigns value to that baby. Analogous to this is the conclusion of Western philosophy: since there is no God, people have no God-given purpose. The only purpose anyone has is that which they create for themselves.

Atheists see this as the responsibility of the individual. In

---

14 Although this work of art shown here depicts despair, the artist may have been portraying his own experience unrelated to the despair induced by a philosophical realization that nothing has meaning.

fact, Western philosophy ends with a call to wake up! Stop being in despair. Stop being a victim. Accept responsibility for your own meaning. Create yourself. Since there is no God, you must be God for yourself.

How then should people exist? "Authentically." By this, philosophers mean the individual should do what they are designed to do. The apple tree produces apples. The dog barks and wags its tail. The architect designs buildings. The artist creates art. To live in accordance with that which is inside oneself, and to live it passionately and sincerely, is to live authentically.

Today many outside of the philosophical world use the term "authentic," but this and many other common words were coined in the context of philosophers communicating their values.

Living authentically is the best Western atheism can offer. Nothing else makes sense. And philosophically-speaking, even living authentically does not make sense because nothing has meaning.

Point 2.12: Atheism Offers a Throne

Within the home of atheism there is a throne upon which each resident gets to sit. It is a throne from where the individual can govern their own life. They must govern their own life because no one else can or will.

It is a throne elevated above the masses, a position from where it is clear that everyone else is enslaved to traditional and religious values.

It is a throne from where God, Jesus, or any divine being

is seen as a delusion. It is a throne from where the Christian idea of acknowledging Jesus as Lord is seen as foolishness and bondage.

Atheism is a perspective. It is a way of looking down at the world and knowing that you are the sovereign king of your own life.

ATHEISM IS A PERSPECTIVE OF SOVEREIGNTY OVER ONE'S LIFE

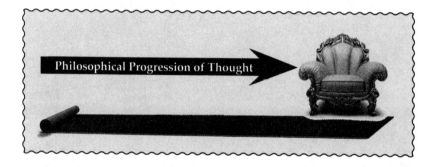

Philosophical Progression of Thought

Summary of Section Two

The historic Western philosophical progression influences everyone in the Western world to some degree but it is aggressively imposed upon young minds in our secular universities.

Unfortunately, most Christian parents are unaware. After spending 18 or more years, loving, praying for, and training their children to embrace a set of values based on God, they will send their children off to an institution which has, as its goal, to remold young minds according to its image. Parents will pay universities significant life-savings to reprogram their children.

But it is not only universities that promote this fundamental worldview. Western education is influenced to some degree at all levels. Although there are countless wonderful teachers doing their best to teach reading, writing, and arithmetic, most of those teachers were trained in the secular university system under the influence of Western philosophy. As a result, most are unaware of how open they are to receive and pass on small bites of the philosophical message.

The values that correspond with the philosophical progression are passed on to the masses through every form of communication: phrases, clichés, and thoughts delivered through YouTube, Facebook, blogs, a new best-selling book, a heart-gripping movie, a popular song, an intellectual interviewed on television, a university student visiting home during spring break, a work of art, a poem, comments made while drinking at a bar, or a discussion at the local coffee shop.

Those who become indoctrinated will conclude God is unprovable, faith is irrational, and religion is the abode of the naive, weak-minded individual. They will treat nothing as sacred, and so, traditional values associated with life, sex, and marriage will vanish. Seeing all individuals as sovereign, they will identify evil people as those who impose their values on or oppress others via their financial advantages, religious rules, or governmental laws. In the end, they will come into agreement with the cultural and political values common to others who build on the foundation of atheism /agnosticism.

Even students trained in our Christian universities often come out with similar values because the Western philosophical progression is so all-pervasive in the modern Western world of higher education.

Those who drink the Kool-Aid will step into freedom from rules, then into despair, then into nihilism. For a time they will wander, trying on different lifestyles, but eventually anchor their life in some north star separate from God. Then, if they hope to cope successfully, they will have to create their own world, a world in which they will have to imagine their life has meaning.

Millions of people in the Western world have embraced the whole package of values that corresponds to the atheistic worldview. They have built their lives on those values. But remember, atheism cannot be proven. As explained in Section 1, no one can prove God's non-existence. Therefore, the values built on that foundation have no foundation.

Section Three

Exchanging Assumptions
With Hypotheses

The historic Western philosophical progression is built on several seriously flawed assumptions, two of which we will identify in this section. Then we will replace those two assumptions with two concepts taught in the Bible.

Of course, some readers have rejected the Bible, thinking it is full of errors and irrelevant, so they will be skeptical of the two concepts that I will take from those pages. But even if you think the Bible has errors, that does not mean everything in the book is wrong. Millions of people have been finding some wisdom in there throughout the last two millennia.

Besides, I will not expect you to accept the two biblically-derived concepts as true. Instead, I will propose them as two hypotheses in the same way hypotheses are used in the scientific method. As explained earlier, a hypothesis is "a proposed explanation made on the basis of limited evidence as a starting point for further investigation."[15] Those who use the scientific methods put forth a hypothesis, then continue studying and experimenting to see if the hypothesis can accurately predict future results. The more reliably the hypothesis predicts future results, the more trust that can be placed in that hypothesis.

---

15 From the *Oxford Living Dictionary*.

Exchanging Assumptions with Hypotheses

So I will not be asking you to blindly accept what the Bible says. Instead, I will propose two concepts from the Bible that will serve as hypotheses to replace two assumptions at the foundation of Western philosophical thought. Two hypotheses will replace two assumptions.

I will refer to the two concepts at the foundation of Western philosophy as "assumptions" (rather than "hypotheses") because I have never heard of philosophy students being encouraged to question either of the assumptions identified in this section. In contrast, I am asking you to question and test the hypotheses at the foundation of a progression of thought leading to theism.

Then we will compare the Western philosophical progression of thought leading to atheism / agnosticism with the progression of thought built on the biblically-derived hypotheses leading to theism.

Point 3.1: Plato's First Assumption

Let's begin by using our epistemological skills on the contributions of Plato that we identified in Section 1. As explained, Plato contributed the fundamental cosmology at the foundation of Western civilization. He taught that there are two worlds—a spiritual world and a natural world. Plato envisioned his spiritual world as eternally existing and located above the natural world.

PLATO'S COSMOLOGY:
SPIRITUAL WORLD AND NATURAL WORLD

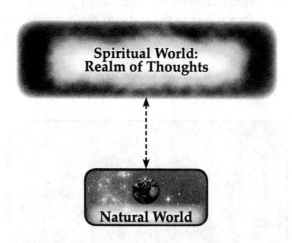

Where did Plato get this cosmology? Certainly, Plato is correct that there is a natural world around us—we can see it. But what about the spiritual world? Plato never claimed to have seen the spiritual world. He assumed its existence and location outside of and beyond the natural world. Plato's cosmology is the assumption at the foundation of Western philosophy.

Exchanging Assumptions with Hypotheses

Point 3.2: A Biblically-Derived Cosmology

Let's replace Plato's cosmology with a cosmology derived from the Bible. The first verse in the Bible tells us:

In the beginning God created the heavens and the earth.
Genesis 1:1

This tells us God not only created the earth, but also the "heavens." This identifies the fundamental difference between the cosmology of Plato and the cosmology derived from the Bible.[16] Let me explain.

The Bible uses the words "heaven" and "heavens" interchangeably. When either word, singular or plural, is used in the Bible, it most often refers to the *natural regions* we see when we look up into the sky, including the clouds, planets, and stars.[17]

BIBLICAL COSMOLOGY:
WITH THE NATURAL HEAVENS WITHIN CREATION

The Bible also associates the terms "heaven" and "heavens" with the *invisible, spiritual realm*. However, we should not

---

16 The differences between these two cosmologies are explained in depth in another book I have written entitled, *Father-Son Theology*.

17 This use of the words "heaven" and "heavens" is confirmed in many Bible verses, including, Genesis 1:9, 1:14-15, and Psalm 8:8.

envision the spiritual realm as separated from and high above the natural realm, as Plato's cosmology does. According to Genesis 1:1 (quoted above), all the heavens are created. In other words, the heavens are within creation. This idea of both the natural and spiritual heavens being part of creation is stated or implied in many Bible passages.[18]

In order to develop this understanding of the spiritual realm being within creation, allow me for a moment to diagram the spiritual realm as a flat plane located behind another flat plan representing the natural realm. The natural realm is shown in front of the spiritual realm because it helps us think of the natural realm as the realm that is visible to us. At the same time, the spiritual realm is shown behind the natural realm, representing how the spiritual realm is hidden from our natural senses.

BIBLICAL COSMOLOGY:
NATURAL REALM SUPERIMPOSED UPON THE SPIRITUAL REALM

Seeing creation as two separate planes with one superimposed upon the other is helpful, but may mislead people to think there is a distance between the natural and spiritual realms. In reality, they fill the same space. Therefore, I will make

---

18 A few of those confirming passages are Psalm 33:6, Nehemiah 9:6, 2 Kings 19:15, Isaiah 45:12, and Revelation 10:6.

another adaptation in our diagram by enclosing all of creation in "one package."

This is the biblically-derived cosmology. The natural and spiritual realms are *within creation,* and they *fill the same space.*[19]

Point 3.3: The Location of God's Throne

At this point, I am not trying to convince anyone that the biblically-derived cosmology is true. I am simply explaining how the people who wrote the Bible understood the nature of the world. What was their cosmology? And how did it differ from Plato's cosmology?

There are many passages in the Bible that reveal how the Bible writers understood that the spiritual realm filled the natural realm.

---

19 The natural and spiritual realms are both within creation, but to be technically accurate, we would not say the natural and spiritual realms *completely* fill the same space. Deeper thought leads the Bible reader to envision the spiritual realm as bigger than the natural realm. Therefore, it may be more accurate to say that the spiritual realm fills the natural realm and extends beyond it with size and/or additional dimensions.

This is most evident when we consider how God is shown in the Bible as filling creation. Jeremiah spoke from God's perspective saying, "Do I not fill the heavens and the earth?" (Jeremiah 23:24). In what form does God exist within creation? John 4:24 tells us God is spirit. Hence, we see God in a spiritual state filling the spiritual and natural realms.[20]

BIBLICAL COSMOLOGY:
GOD ENTERED INTO[21] AND FILLS THE HEAVENS AND EARTH

Even though the Bible reveals God filling creation, it also talks about people looking "upwards" to Him. When we think of that upward direction we should not envision a separate world located outside of and above creation (as Plato's cosmology portrays). The Bible shows the throne of God located within creation. The Psalmist declares:

The Lord has established His throne in the heavens . . .

(Ps. 103:19)

---

20 In some passages we can see God temporarily revealing himself in physical form, e.g., Genesis 32:28-30, but on a continual basis God's existence within creation is in spiritual form.

21 "Entered into" may be inaccurate terminology, because a biblically-derived cosmology may also envision God filling creation as it came into existence, rather than entering into it after it was created.

Exchanging Assumptions with Hypotheses

Notice this is *not* talking about a throne that preexisted creation. This is a throne that had a beginning and was "established" at a point in time in the heavens which are part of creation (see also, 1 Kings 22:19; Ps. 11:4; Is. 66:1; Matt. 5:34).[22]

This is a cosmology with God filling creation, yet at the same time having a throne within creation. However, the throne of God is spiritual and, therefore, cannot be tied to any one location within the natural realm. It is more accurate to think of the throne as existing in a spiritual dimension in which "upward" signifies higher in authority, grandeur, and majesty, rather than physical location.

BIBLICAL COSMOLOGY: GOD'S THRONE WITHIN CREATION

This is the biblically-derived cosmology that we will be talking about and contrasting to Plato's cosmology throughout the rest of this book.

---

22 Another reason we must understand the biblically-derived cosmology with God's throne within creation, rather than outside of the natural world as Plato's cosmology depicts, is because the changing of time within the throne room is evident in many Bible passages. For example, angels and people go in and out of God's throne room, which would be logically impossible if God's throne room was located in a timeless, uncreated world as Plato's cosmology depicts. For in depth teaching on this see another book I have written entitled, *Father-Son Theology*.

Point 3.4: The Spiritual and Natural Realms Are Integrated

The Bible writers saw the natural and spiritual realms as interrelated. Paul wrote about Jesus' relationship with the world:

> *For in Him all things were created, both in the heavens and on earth, visible and invisible . . . He is before all things, and in Him all things hold together.*
>
> Colossians 1:16-17

Paul, the writer, held to a cosmology in which Jesus holds all things—in heaven and on earth, visible and invisible—together. That cosmology leads us to conclude that creation would cease to exist, as we know it, if Jesus' influence was removed from creation. From this, we can infer that the natural and spiritual realms influence each other and are *interrelated* in some fashion.

For another example consider the Bible passages that reveal how spiritual beings manifested and influenced the natural realm. Angels which exist in the spiritual realm, sometimes "materialized" in the sense of taking on physical form, i.e., Hebrews 13:2. The Bible writers held that the natural and spiritual realms were not completely separated, but rather they influence each other.

Also, consider how the Bible writers envisioned God's spirit sustaining life in every human being. The writer of Job explained this about God:

> *If He should determine to do so,*
> *If He should gather to Himself His spirit and His breath,*
> *All flesh would perish together,*
> *And man would return to dust.*
>
> Job 34:14-15

71

Exchanging Assumptions with Hypotheses

According to this Bible passage, every human being depends upon the spirit and breath of God to be alive. Removing God's spirit would cause all of humanity to die and turn to dust, which shows the natural and spiritual realms *integrated* with each other at least in some fashion.

To summarize, the biblically-derived cosmology sees that God created one world and within that one world are the heavens—both the natural heavens (atmosphere and outer space) and the spiritual heavens (invisible realm).

Accurate terminology helps understanding. It would be misleading to refer to a natural "world" and a spiritual "world" (as Plato did). Instead, a biblically-derived cosmology identifies one created world with two "realms." This means the biblical cosmology is not dualistic as Plato's cosmology is. By referring to Plato's cosmology as dualistic, we mean Plato imagined two worlds, a spiritual world existing separated from and far above the natural world. In contrast, the biblically-derived cosmology sees one world with a natural realm and spiritual realm filling the same space and integrated with each other.[23]

Point 3.5: Exchange Plato's for Paul's Cosmology

Now I ask you to exchange Plato's dualistic cosmology with the biblically-derived cosmology. Remember, I am not expecting you to blindly accept the biblically-derived cosmology. Instead, I am presenting it as a hypothesis. Before we can test it, we must make the exchange in our thoughts.

---

23 It would be wrong to say the two realms are *fully* integrated because deeper thought leads the Bible reader to envision the spiritual realm much bigger than the natural realm. It may be more accurate to say that the spiritual realm intrudes into the natural realm or that the natural realm is a subset of the spiritual realm.

SWITCHING FROM PLATO'S COSMOLOGY TO THE
BIBLICALLY-DERIVED COSMOLOGY

Some readers may have a difficult time seriously considering the biblically-derived cosmology because they have already rejected the Bible and, therefore, have a general bias against anything written in those pages. For them, it may be easier if I refer to the biblically-derived cosmology as "Paul's cosmology." Paul wrote much of the New Testament, and if I accredit the cosmology to an individual like Paul, it is easier to see it as a possibly true cosmology just as much as Plato's cosmology is possibly true. Plato was a human being. Paul was a human being. Either could have been correct. Either or both could have been wrong.

To add a few points to Paul's credibility, it is worth noting that Paul was highly educated, well-trained in the ancient Greek philosophers' teaching, plus Hebraic thinking, and Christian thought. In contrast, Plato could not have been aware of Paul's cosmology since he lived over 300 years before Paul and there are no historical records that Plato was ever educated in Hebraic thought.

Paul's cosmology could be accurately referred to by other names, including, "Moses' cosmology", "David's cosmology", "Mathew's cosmology", "John's cosmology", "Jesus' cosmology", etc.[24] The biblically-derived cosmology was built on Genesis 1:1. It is at the foundation of thought throughout the Bible. As far as we know, all 40 plus Bible writers understood the natural and spiritual realms to be part of creation and integrated with one another.

Point 3.6: The Dominant Cosmology Worldwide

Today, most people who live where Western culture and education are dominant, hold to a dualistic cosmology structured like Plato's. They may not include God in their cosmology, but they tend to envision a spiritual world located separate from and above the natural world.

Outside of those regions under Western influence, most people in the world hold to a cosmology similar to Paul's cosmology. They may not included God in their cosmology, but they envision the natural and spiritual realms filling the same space and integrated with each other.

For example, most people on the continent of Africa are very conscious of an invisible, spiritual realm that is very close to and integrated with the natural realm. The billion plus people in India are influenced by the Hindu and Buddhist worldviews and are, therefore, ever aware of spiritual forces determined by

---

24 Unfortunately, I cannot accurately refer to this as the "Christian cosmology," because Western Christianity has been profoundly influenced by Plato's cosmology. For those interested in this, I have written extensively on this subject in another book entitled, *Father-Son Theology*.

karma and other spiritual dynamics. Most of the billion plus people in China are ever conscious of *ch'i,* which to them is the basic stuff of the cosmos, which is thought of as matter-energy or vital force. To most Chinese people, *ch'i* permeates all things that exist in the natural realm. Most people living in under-developed regions also think of physical things as charged with spiritual energy, whether we are speaking of a mountain, tree, or bird. When all these people groups are taken into account, we realize the majority of humanity today holds to a cosmology that acknowledges a spiritual realm that is close to and integrated with the natural realm.

This is not stated to imply that we should embrace the biblically-derived cosmology just because it is the majority view. That is not my purpose in mentioning this. Rather, I just want to overcome the misconceptions many people have about the Western philosophical view. Sometimes proponents of Western thought make others who disagree feel like they are alone in their viewpoint. In reality, Plato's cosmology is only dominant where Western culture and education has been dominant.

Point 3.7: The Beginning Determines the End

Which cosmology we start with—Paul's or Plato's—profoundly influences the conclusion at which we finally arrive. Individuals trained in logic know well the truth that the beginning usually determines the end. It is sometimes expressed by saying, "He who frames the argument wins the argument."

In the Western world, philosophers have been framing the argument for hundreds of years. They start with the assumption of Plato's cosmology. Then Western philosophy creates a greater and greater separation between the spiritual and natural

Exchanging Assumptions with Hypotheses

worlds. It continues distancing God from the individual then totally isolates God from the natural world or even dismisses God as non-existent.

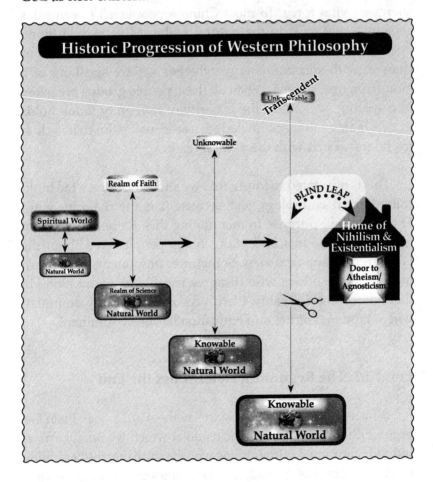

In contrast, a progression of thought starting with the biblically-derived cosmology cannot separate God from the natural world. God fills the heavens and earth. He has a throne within creation. So if we start with a cosmology that only has one world and God fills that one world, we will end with theism. Start with theism—end with theism.

The Biblically-Derived Cosmology:
Begins and Ends with God Filing Creation

However, it would be a huge over-simplification of the whole argument about the existence of God if we started with God filling the world. I don't want to make it that easy. I want to show you how a logical progression of thought, starting with biblically-derived hypotheses leads to theism. Therefore, for the sake of showing how a logical progression leads to theism, let just say we don't know if God fills the natural realm. Let's remove that element of the biblically-derived cosmology. Then, we can see if we still arrive at theism.

The Biblically-Derived Cosmology:
The Spiritual and Natural Realms Integrated

With this biblically-derived cosmology, there is still only one world with two realms. Those two realms are integrated.

Exchanging Assumptions with Hypotheses

Point 3.8: Plato's Cosmology is the Hidden Rabbit

In the previous point, we stated how our starting cosmology determines our final conclusion. This is evident in Western philosophy which starts with the assumption of Plato's cosmology. That assumption predetermines the conclusion of atheism / agnosticism.

To see this, realize Plato's cosmology starts with *God excluded from the natural world*. Plato's cosmology only allows God to exist in a distant world totally unlike the natural world. Therefore, if philosophers move that spiritual world further and further away, they are moving God further and further away. Get rid of the spiritual world and they have gotten rid of God. That is exactly what Western philosophy has done over the course of 2,400 years.

In this sense, Plato's cosmology is like the rabbit hidden in the hat of the magician. The philosopher starts with Plato's cosmology, then adds 2,400 years of argument, and in the end pulls the rabbit out the hat. Abracadabra! Atheism / agnosticism!

Of course, no philosopher would like being compared to a magician, and with that comparison, I am over-simplifying the case. Yet, almost all Western philosophers have the magic rabbit—Plato's cosmology—at the foundation of their thoughts.

Starting with Paul's (biblically-derived) cosmology completely undermines the Western philosophical separation of the spiritual and natural worlds. That separation is impossible if we start with Paul's cosmology that sees the spiritual and natural realms filling the same space and integrated.

Point 3.9: Embracing Paul's Cosmology

Again, I am not expecting you to blindly accept Paul's cosmology. At this point, I hope you will seriously consider it, begin testing it, and think about where it will lead you.

Paul's cosmology does not require a huge stretch of the imagination. Since it sees the spiritual realm integrated with the natural realm, it allows for spiritual forces acting upon the natural realm. Such dynamics may explain many experiences that Plato's cosmology cannot explain.

For example, one time I was involved in a discussion with students of Western philosophy. Most of them said they were atheists but during the course of the discussion, one young man in the group talked about an event in his life that he was unable to explain as an entirely natural phenomenon. The event he explained seemed more than coincidental. The young atheist could not explain it, so he was seriously considering if some spiritual force orchestrated the related events to bring about what he experienced.

After this young man told about his experience, almost every person involved in the discussion admitted they had also experienced some phenomenon that seemed to have required another force beyond what we know about the natural world.

Such experiences are common. In 2009, the Gallup organization asked Americans if they had ever had "a religious or mystical experience" and 49 percent said yes.[25] In 2000, a survey was conducted by David Hay in the UK and over 75 percent of respondents said they were "aware of a spiritual dimension to their experience."[26]

---

25 http://www.philosophyforlife.org/the-spiritual-experiences-survey/ Retrieved April 2019.
26 Ibid.

Exchanging Assumptions with Hypotheses

I mention this not to try to prove that there is a spiritual realm integrated into the natural realm. That is not my intent. Rather, I mention this to help readers realize a cosmology like Paul's is not irrational. Many people, including atheists, have had experiences that they have not been able to explain while building on Plato's cosmology.

Point 3.10: Assumption 2—Intellect Is the Control Center

Earlier, I stated that we will identify two assumptions at the foundation of Western philosophy and then exchange those assumptions for two biblically-derived hypotheses. We have identified the first assumption of Western philosophy—Plato's dualistic cosmology which excludes God from the natural world. Now let's go on to talk about the other assumption.

A second assumption of Western philosophy is that the intellect[27] is the control center of a person's being. That assumption goes back to Socrates and Plato. With Socrates, logic was considered a function of the intellect, and he saw logic as the judge of all that is true. Plato built on Socrates' assumption, but he reinforced it by teaching that people's thoughts give them access to the world of the spirit, all truth, and ultimately god (as he conceived of god).

Trust in the human intellect became seated in Western philosophy in the 13th century when Thomas Aquinas taught that the heart of humanity is fallen (corrupt and prone to sin) but the intellect is able to arrive at truth. This was in contrast to Augustine who taught that both the heart and intellect of humanity are fallen (corrupt and prone to sin).

---

27 I am using the word, "intellect," rather than "mind," because the word "mind" has a different definition for those holding to a biblical cosmology than those who hold to Plato's cosmology. In contrast, the intellect refers to the faculty of reasoning and understanding, regardless of which of the two cosmologies a person holds.

Many leaders ran with Aquinas' conclusion, placing trust in their intellect, which gave a launching pad for the Scientific Revolution of the 16th and 17th centuries. Positive developments came forth once people began to confidently use their reasoning powers to solve problems. However, the severing of the intellect from the heart allowed Western philosophy to move down a darkened path. This will become evident as we continue.

Point 3.11: Hypothesis 2—The Heart Is the Control Center

As an alternative to the philosophical assumption that the *intellect* is the control center, consider what the Bible tells us about the central role the *heart* plays in governing a person's life. Proverbs 4:23 tells us:

> *Watch over your heart with all diligence,*
> *For from it flow the springs of life.*
>
> Proverbs 4:23

Jesus also talked about the words and actions of people proceeding from their heart (Matthew 15:17-20). Other verses state or imply that the human conscience is seated in the heart, and hence, the heart plays the key role in revealing to a person what is right and what is wrong (1 John 3:20; Hebrews 10:22).

There are other Bible passages that reveal the pivotal role the heart plays in human life but perhaps the strongest evidence comes from passages showing the heart as a person's primary contact point with God. This is in contrast to Plato's understanding that people have contact with the world of the spirit and god through the thoughts of their mind. The Bible writers tell us God watches over the heart of each person (Jeremiah 17:10; 1 Samuel 16:7) and Jesus' spirit comes into the heart of the believer (Gal. 4:6).

Exchanging Assumptions with Hypotheses

These Bible passages do not translate into the idea that the heart *completely controls* a person's thoughts and behavior. Rather, the Bible writers saw that the heart strongly *influences* and *guides* thoughts and behavior. However, to simplify this discussion, I am going to refer to the heart as the "control center of human nature" so I can easily contrast it to the Western assumption that the intellect is the control center of human nature.

Philosophical Assumption	Biblically-derived Hypothesis
Intellect	Heart
is the control center	is the control center

Remember, we are not expecting anyone to blindly accept the biblically-derived hypothesis. Rather we are simply identifying the understanding of people who wrote the Bible so we can use their understanding as a hypothesis and an alternative to the assumption of Western philosophy.

Point 3.12: Integrated Natural and Spiritual Realms

When we talk about the heart as the control center, we are not referring to the physical organ pumping blood throughout the physical body. To understand the heart from the perspective of those who wrote the Bible, we must first embrace the biblically-derived cosmology. Once we see the natural and spiritual realms as integrated, we can see human nature as integrated into the natural and spiritual realms. In other words, a person exists in both the natural and spiritual realms.

People who embrace the biblically-derived understanding of human nature usually refer to the invisible part of human nature that exists in the spiritual world as the "soul."

There are many different ways to understand human nature. Even Evangelical Christians who all claim to build their understanding on the Bible vary in their views. Some make distinctions between the soul and spirit. Others assign various functions to the spirit, but not to the soul. I have taught in depth on those views in another book entitled, *Father-Son Theology.* Here an in depth understanding of human nature is not relevant to our discussion on whether or not God exists. Therefore, I will simplify the following discussion by only referring to the human soul and the human body.

To those who wrote the Bible, the soul is the same size and shape as the physical body. Plus, the soul is structured like the body. This understanding of the human soul is evident in many Bible passages. Most clearly, it is seen in passages describing a person after they have died, when their physical body has been removed and they continue to exist as a soul.

HUMAN NATURE INTEGRATED INTO THE NATURAL AND SPIRITUAL REALMS

For example, consider an experience Jesus' disciples had when Peter was taken to prison, then later escaped.[28] Peter came to the door where the disciples were gathered, but they did not immediately allow him to enter. They thought Peter may have already been put to death, so they were not sure if the person

---

28 Acts 12:13-15.

standing outside of their door was Peter still alive or if it was his ghost (soul). In other words, they expected his soul and his body to look identical.

For another example, consider the story Jesus told about a rich man who lived in opulence and a poor man named Lazarus who suffered greatly while alive. Jesus explained how after they died they both went to a placed called hades. There Lazarus was held in a region of blessings while the rich man was held in a region of suffering. Even though neither had physical bodies while in hades, Jesus described how the rich man asked if Lazarus could take a drop of water on his finger and touch the rich man's tongue.[29] Jesus' description implies that people have the same parts (such as fingers and a tongue) even after they are separated from their physical body.

To the people who lived in Jesus' day, such reports about the afterlife were thought of as true. The point being, they held that people had a soul structured like their physical body.

There are other reports in the Bible that reveal this understanding of human nature. Here I just need you to comprehend how people who lived when the Bible was written understood a person's entire being consisting of both spiritual and natural substances, plus those spiritual and natural substances are integrated with each other

Point 3.13: The Integrated Heart

Once we recognize human nature as integrated, we can also see the heart as integrated into the natural and spiritual realms.

In order to understand the function of the spiritual heart, it is necessary to think in terms of metaphors. The physical

---

29 Luke 16:19-24.

heart is the pump for the blood that collects oxygen and food, then distributes the related chemicals throughout the person's physical body. In a metaphorical sense, we can say the spiritual heart is the fountainhead of life. For this reason, the writer of Proverbs tells that from the heart "flow the springs of life" (Proverbs 4:23). It is accurate to think of the spiritual heart as the inner core of a person's being from where the person's strength, will, and personality flow.

HUMAN HEART[30] INTEGRATED INTO THE
NATURAL AND SPIRITUAL REALMS

This biblically-derived understanding of the heart also sees the heart as—the seat of desires, affections, love, faith, hope, and purpose.[31]

Point 3.14: Testing the Second Hypothesis

Now it is time to make the switch from the second assumption at the foundation of Western philosophy (the

---

30 Of course, the human heart is not shaped as diagramed here. We are simply using a symbol often used to represent the human heart.

31 This understanding is derived from many Bible passages including, Matthew 5:28, Romans 10:10, Acts 11:23, and 2 Corinthians 9:7.

Exchanging Assumptions with Hypotheses

intellect is the control center) to the second biblically-derived hypothesis (the heart is the control center). Once we make the switch, we can test the hypothesis to see if it more accurately predicts human behavior.

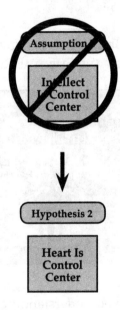

A hypothesis deserves a lifetime of testing, which of course, we cannot do in these few pages. However, we can consider a few real-life experiences that reveal much. Consider the following examples of individuals and how their thoughts are guided and influenced by their heart.

A college student named Justin has fallen in love with his neighbor, Huī yīn. As a result, Justin's thoughts are being guided as to how he can please Huī yīn. In other words, Justin's heart is guiding his thoughts.

Has God Proven His Existence?

Ahmad is a Muslim with a deep faith in Allah. As a result, his thoughts are being aligned toward doing what he believes is Allah's will.

Jamie holds unforgiveness and bitterness in his heart toward his ex-wife, Lynn. As a result, it does not matter what Lynn does, Jamie interprets her actions as intended to destroy him.

Leah desires in her heart (the seat of desires) to find and purchase a new car. As a result, her intellect has been at work accumulating information necessary to secure the new car. So in this case, Leah's heart activates her intellect and her intellect is a servant of her heart.

Each of these examples are made-up, but we all know real situations similar to these that do reveal how the heart influences the intellect.

In recent years, there has been extensive psychological research done in a related field of study known as "confirmation bias." This refers to the tendency of people to search out, interpret, and remember concepts that support what they already believe.

For an example of confirmation bias, think of Corey who believes that people of a certain ethic group are inferior and prone to evil. As a consequence, Corey tends to find and retain evidence to reinforce his belief. Corey even gathers information about other people that may be entirely imagined, and he incorporates that information into his memory and thought patterns.

Adisa believes the world is getting worse and worse, so she selectively hears and remembers news about how terrible society is. Adisa's friend, Javier, believes the world is getting better and better, so he consciously and subconsciously collects news bits about how good the world is.

Exchanging Assumptions with Hypotheses

None of these examples *prove* the heart is the control center of human nature, but they do provide some evidence that such things as love, faith, and desires, do influence thoughts.

Through my own continued investigation of this subject, I have become convinced the biblically-derived hypothesis (the heart is the control center) predicts human behavior more accurately than the assumption of Western philosophy (the intellect is the control center). Discerning readers will continue to test this hypothesis and come to their own conclusion.

Point 3.15: Can the Intellect Be Trusted?

The second assumption of Western philosophy that we have identified leads one to think that the intellect can arrive at truth independently of the heart. In contrast, Hypothesis 2, that the heart is the control center, leads one to think that the intellect should not be trusted without the correct guidance of the heart.

Let me qualify this. The intellect can collect true information, such as the facts that the sky is blue and Jupiter is a planet. With Hypothesis 2, we are not talking about collecting such data. Instead, we are talking about the truths of life associated with the big questions people ask, such as:

1. Does God exist?
2. Why do I exist?
3. Is there life after death?
4. What is right versus wrong?

Hypothesis 2 leads us to conclude that the human intellect, without the correct guidance of the heart, should not be trusted to arrive at truths that answer such important, life-forming questions.[32] Consider an example related to the existence of God.

Point 3.16: The Heart Guides the Questions

Devin and Sean are adults who were raised in a traditional church and had experiences in their younger years that they each considered were from God. As Devin and Sean matured, they independently began asking questions about God.

Deep in his heart, Devin wanted to continue following God, and he asked himself, "Is it possible my earlier experiences actually were from God?"

In contrast, Sean *did not* want to continue following God, and he asked himself, "Is it possible my earlier experiences were merely psychological phenomena?"

Both Devin and Sean answered their own question in the affirmative, which is a reasonable answer in each of their cases.

Devin and Sean continued to ask more questions.

Devin went on to ask himself, "Since my earlier experiences may have been truly of God, do I have proof that God exists?"

At the same time, Sean asked himself, "Since my earlier experiences may have been entirely psychological, do I have any proof that God exists?"

Devin concluded he may have proof of God's existence, while Sean concluded he has no proof of God's existence.

---

32 This biblically-derived understanding of the heart's role in guiding the intellect is evident in such Bible passages as Jeremiah 17:9 and Ephesians 4:17-18.

Exchanging Assumptions with Hypotheses

Each of their conclusions was aligned with what was already in their heart.

Devin and Sean then asked themselves if they have any basis for morality. Devin reasoned God may have proven his existence, and therefore, he should govern his life according to God's will.

In contrast, Sean reasoned God has given him no proof of his existence, and therefore, he has no unwavering standard for determining right from wrong.

Over the course of several months, Devin and Sean asked and answered dozens of related questions for themselves. As a result, they each developed an entire progression of thought. They both started in the same place: an experience that may have been from God. However, they ended at different conclusions.

Both Devin and Sean were convinced they arrived at logical answers to each of the questions they asked themselves. But what they missed was that the progression of thoughts they each developed was guided by their questions more than their answers.

To see this, look again at Devin's and Sean's first question:

Devin: "Is it possible that my earlier experiences actually were from God?"

Sean: "Is it possible that my earlier experiences were merely psychological phenomena?"

These questions were designed to lead to specific answers.

Most questions have a predetermined direction. This is because questions originate in the desire to know something.

Since the heart is the seat of desires, the heart influences the questions. We each have a tendency to engineer questions that will lead us where we want to go.

Devin and Sean were unaware of this. They assumed questions are neutral, not leading one way or another. They did not "question their questions."

Point 3.17: Answers Come from Chasing Bones

There are some very simple questions that may be neutral. For example, a child may ask her parent, "How do bananas grow?" Such a question is raised out of a desire to know something, but it is not necessarily biased in the sense of hoping for a predetermined answer.

However, most questions are, at least in part, motivated by some desired answer. Often the desired answer is hidden, unknown by the person asking the question or the person answering.

Answers may also be biased, but it is easier to identify the bias within an answer. Therefore, people are more careful when giving answers. Then they try to be logical. But they are not as careful when asking questions because they rarely recognize the bias in questions.

Recently, there was a government shutdown in our country because two political parties refused to finance ongoing government operations until the other side was willing to compromise. During that period, political surveys were being taken and a pollster telephoned my home, asking, "Who do you blame for the shutdown?" That was a biased question because it assumed people "blame" someone for the shutdown. The question could have been biased in the opposing direction by wording it this way: "Who do you give *credit* for the shutdown?"

The political pollster's question was designed to steer my answer down a predetermined path. Asking a biased question is like "throwing a bone." The question casts a bone in one direction or another. The person answering typically doesn't question the question because they are quick to chase the bone.

Point 3.18: Critical Thinking Can Be Deceptive

One of the most seductive ways of steering questions has become known as "critical thinking."

On the positive side, critical thinking can be a great benefit in revealing truth. At the foundation of critical thinking is Socrates' teaching that we can never know if our ideas are true until we ask the right questions—the questions that reveal false assumptions and illogical steps in our thought progression. Indeed, Socrates gave us a helpful tool to distinguish truth from error. His approach has been developed and refined over the last 2,400 years and was assigned the label "critical thinking," in the mid-late 20th century.

Today, there are different types of critical thinking and many forms can be very beneficial. For example, elementary school teachers often instruct their students to ask questions about what they are reading. Those questions help the children find clues that reveal what the author is trying to say. Indeed, the tools of critical thinking can help people clarify the thoughts of others and their own thoughts.

However, critical thinking can also be used to manipulate the thoughts of others. For example, Jennifer and Carlos were participating in a group discussion, and Jennifer made a statement that contradicted what Carlos said. The group leader intervened, but in that intervention, she directed the group to think critically about Jennifer's comment. The leader thought she was being totally neutral, but everyone is biased in some way. The leader guided the group's critical thinking toward revealing the errors in Jennifer's progression of thought because she disagreed with Jennifer. At the same time, she did not direct the group to think critically about what Carlos said because she agreed with Carlos and, therefore, could not even see the errors in Carlos' thought processes.

Critical thinking often directs listeners to assign motives to another individual. For example, a discussion may begin about what the president of the country is doing. Then, the leader of the discussion, who does not approve of the president, may ask, "Why do you suppose the president did that?" If someone proposes a positive motive, the discussion leader may ask another question, such as, "Is it possible that the president had some other motive?" The leader can continue along this line of questioning until someone proposes some sinister motive. Using such questions, the leader can "help" everyone see things from the leader's perspective and eventually conclude that the president is not such a good person.

Similar dynamics occur when discussing any subject for which there are two or more viewpoints. Whoever leads the critical thinking guides the questions. Questions are usually guided by the heart.

Point 3.19: Corollary Assumptions

We identified the second assumption of Western philosophy as *the intellect is the control center of human nature.*

Exchanging Assumptions with Hypotheses

The Second Assumption of Western Philosophy
The intellect is the control center of human nature.

This philosophical assumption leads to many corollary concepts. These concepts are not all direct implications, but they are related ideas that we have been discussing. For example, we explained how Western philosophy separated the intellect from the heart when Aquinas said the heart of man is fallen (corrupt and prone to sin) but the intellect is not.

1. The heart of humanity is fallen but the intellect is not

Once Western philosophy separated the intellect from the fallen heart, the intellect was accepted as trustworthy.

2. The intellect can be trusted to arrive at truth

Closely associated with this is the idea that logic always leads to truth.

3. If a progression of the thought is logical, it is true

Another result of separating the intellect from the heart is the idea that questions originate in the intellect, rather than the heart. Therefore, questions are innocent and neutral. Furthermore, questions open the door to truth.

4. Questions arise from the intellect
5. Questions are innocent and neutral
6. Questions are the door to truth

Someone continuing to build a progression of thought on these concepts may say, "Since questions are the door to truth, no one should be afraid of questions." Then they may add, "No one who is searching for truth should question the questions."

7. No one should be afraid of questions

8. No one should question the questions

I do not mean to present these eight points as unshakable pillars of Western philosophy. Rather I am presenting these in a very general sense. Generally speaking, all of these points lie at the foundation of Western philosophy

Point 3.20: The Darkened Philosophical Path

Envision a philosophy professor standing before a classroom of students. The professor is an atheist, but a well-trained atheist, intelligent and well-respected in the academic community.

That professor has embraced the philosophical division between the intellect and heart. He believes the intellect of humanity is not fallen and can arrive at truth. He believes a progression of thought that is logical leads to truth. These assumptions will never be discussed in the classroom, but they will lie at the foundation of all classroom discussions. The related concepts are assumed.

The students will be told, "Questions open the door to truth, and therefore, no one should be afraid of questions."

Then the professor begins throwing questions before the students. He will use the same questions that he has been using in the classroom for many years. He knows the questions that his favorite philosophers in history asked themselves. The professor will toss those same questions before the students, knowing that any logical student will chase the bones to certain predetermined answers.

Students will be allowed and even encouraged to debate and argue among themselves about the answers to the questions proposed by the professor. The more intense the debate becomes the more intensely the students will focus on developing the most logical answers. Students most desperate to defend their traditional beliefs—which are usually theists—will be most determined to develop logical answers. But the more focused they are on the answers, the less likely it is they will question the questions.

If and when students debate within the classroom, the professor may praise the students for being willing to face the most important questions of life. He may ridicule those who are too cowardly to answer those questions. From time to time, the professor may intervene in discussions and help the students "think critically" for a moment. Of course, thinking critically sounds like an innocent, commendable endeavor. Yet, the professor orients the students down a specific path every time he directs the critical thinking exercise.

Such classroom interactions can be emotionally charged. As adrenalin is pumping through the bloodstream, chemical chain reactions erupt. In such an energized state, ideas are easily embedded in the mind and thought patterns are shifted.

When such classroom discussions are brought to a close, students may feel good about how logical they have been. They may congratulate themselves about their willingness to be honest and face reality by answering tough questions. Like a dog proud of finding a bone, the students may show off to the professor how good they are at arriving at logical answers.

Then, if and when students make a shift from theism to atheism, they may congratulate themselves. Atheists often make the statement: "I became an atheist because I was willing to ask the tough questions." Such self-congratulation is profoundly misdirected. It totally misses the underlying assumption upon which they built—that their intellect is the control center of their being. That assumption comes with the eight corollary concepts / assumptions that we discussed (point 3.18), such as, no one should question the questions. That group of assumptions blinds the atheist from seeing how "asking the tough questions" may lead to predetermined answers. Rarely do students in a classroom realize they arrived at their answer by chasing bones.

Point 3.21: The Biblically-Derived Alternatives

The group of corollary assumptions at the foundation of Western philosophy is in conflict with the second biblically-derived hypothesis and its implications. Recall Hypothesis 2:

Hypothesis 2
The heart is the control center of human nature.

Because the heart is the control center:

1. **It guides the intellect**
2. **The heart cannot be totally separated from the intellect**
3. **The intellect should not be trusted as an unbiased source of truth**
4. **Not all progressions of thought that seem logical are true**
5. **Questions are influenced by the heart**
6. **Not all questions are innocent or neutral**
7. **Not all questions are the door to truth**
8. **Some questions should be questioned**

Thousands of questions could be offered here as examples of questions that are not innocent, not neutral, and should be questioned. Here are three questions, unrelated to our subject of God's existence, but obviously biased in a direction:

Exchanging Assumptions with Hypotheses

"Is it possible that the senator had an evil motivation when he voted the way he did?"

"What is your sexual orientation? I need to know before I decide whether or not to hire you."

"Doesn't it bother you when your spouse lies like that?"

These questions are not innocent or neutral. Truth will be found by questioning these questions, not answering these questions.

Point 3.22: One Progression of Questions Leading to Theism

Now let me propose one of hundreds of progressions of thought that leads to theism rather than atheism. Please know ahead of reading this that I am not offering this as proof of a creator. That is not my intention here. My intention is to show how questions rather than answers steer the progression of thought.[33]

Question 1: If you found a book with over 1,000 pages of written instructions on how to build a robot, would you conclude that someone must be responsible for writing that book?

Logical answer: Yes.

Question 2: Would it be reasonable to conclude that that book wrote itself or was the product of chance, without the help of any outside intelligent input?

Logical answer: No

33 Several similar discussions that lead to theism can be found at:
https://rcg.org/realtruth/articles/140710-001.html
https://rcg.org/books/dge.html   Retreived 5/19.

Question 3: Now let's say you found stacks and stacks of books that had a total of more than one million pages (more than one thousand books each with one thousand pages) with more than three billion letters giving detailed instructions on how to build a human-looking robot—would it be reasonable to conclude that those books were the product of chance, without the help of any outside intelligent input?

Logical answer: No.

Now compare those stacks of books with a human cell. Every cell in the human body has a genetic code with more than three billion letters written in a specific sequence that give instructions on how to build a human being which is much more complicated than any robot.

Question 4: Is it reasonable to think the human cell with that much information came into existence without any outside intelligent input?

Consider also the fact that if a human cell came into existence by chance, without any outside intelligent input, it would have had to invent by chance:

Exchanging Assumptions with Hypotheses

    a. The language in which the three billion letters are written

    b. The means by which those letters can be translated into usable information

    c. The means by which that information can be used to assemble molecules

    d. The means by which energy can be extracted from the environment and used by the cell

    e. The ability to overcome entropy, which is the force that causes all things to become less organized (decay and breakdown)

Scientific fact: There are about 100 trillion (100,000,000,000,000) cells in every human adult, and every one of those cells[34] has the same sequence of three billion letters, with all the instructions necessary to build another human being.

Scientific fact: If all the information written on the genetic material of all the cells *in one human being* was printed in books (with the type being the size of newspaper print), those books could be spread out and would cover every square inch of the surface of the earth.

Questions 5: Is it logical to conclude that that much written information came into existence by chance without the help of any intelligent input?

This series of questions and answers is not given to prove the existence of an intelligent being (God). Rather it is an example of questions and answers that orient a person toward theism. Notice that the questions steer the progression, not the answers. This series of questions and answers is only one of many examples that could be given here.[35]

---

34 The ovaries and sperm are exceptions.

35 One or many progressions of questions and answers may be developed around any of the points of evidence for God's existence discussed in Section 5.

It is difficult to explain how profoundly progressions of thought are guided by questions more than the answers to those questions. It only takes the slightest influence of the heart to bias a question in one direction or another. A series of several biased questions can steer a progression of thought down a seriously biased path. Even if the answers given are logical, the final conclusion is more likely to be predetermined by the questions.

A PROGRESSION OF THOUGHT IS GUIDED PRIMARILY BY THE QUESTIONS

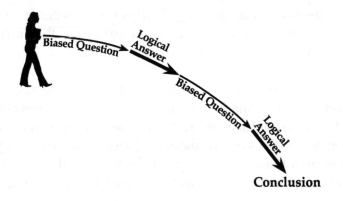

Conclusion

Point 3.23: New Progressions of Thought Are Developed

Every series of related questions and answers develops a progression of thought. The vast majority of progressions people already have in their brain have nothing to do with science or God's existence. They are simply progressions developed so they can make daily decisions.

Many short progressions of thought are developed by advertisers on social media, television, newspapers, magazines, etc. The most effective advertisers are good at asking the question,

Exchanging Assumptions with Hypotheses

"Don't you want this product?" If they make the product look appealing enough, the viewer /listener /reader will "chase the bone," spending a moment thinking about how their life would be better with that product. The resulting progression of thought may form a new neural pathway in their brain eventually leading them to secure that product.

Schools are designed to form in the brain of each student new progressions of thought centered on reading, mathematics, history, government, etc. Teachers work hard at it. They know ahead of time what progressions of thought they need to develop. That is what qualifies them to be instructors. They already know the material. Teachers are prepared to create within the student's brain neural pathways that cause the children to think the way the teacher thinks.

Progressions of thought are also formed by books, movies, works of art, songs, and poems. Even casual conversations between individuals can form new neural pathways resulting in new progressions of thought. Parents also try to replicate their own thought pathways in the brain of their children. If they are skilled at it, they will use more questions than answers.

The result? Everyone has countless progressions of thought already embedded in their brain. Some are beneficial, and some are destructive. Some lead to truth, and some lead to error.

Point 3.24: The Computer Program in the Brain

Progressions of thought function like computer programs. When new data is entered into the computer of a person's brain, the program selectively chooses which data is relevant, then it runs that selected data through the already established pathways. In the end, it spits out the information the program was designed to select, analyze, and organize.

There are thousands of programs people can get for their computer. There are also thousands of progressions of thought they can develop in their brain. But it is important to know that every progression of thought is just that: a progression of thought. It is a program with code written to select data and funnel the selected data down specific pathways.

As thoughts continue running down the same pathways, channels form, steering all future thoughts along the same channels. In time, channels become deep. Those channels may make a person's life easier because the person can readily solve related problems but the channels may also make it difficult for the individual to think independently of their well-established channels.

Apart from some life-changing event, most people will not move their thought patterns out of their present channels.

Point 3.25: My Progression Away from Beauty

I had a progression of thought deeply formed in my brain as a young adult attending university. My first degree was a Bachelor of Science in Wildlife Management. I went into the field because I loved nature. At the university, I eagerly attended classes and got high grades, with hopes of going into a related career.

When I finished that degree, I secured employment helping manage forests. One day while working, I looked up at a mountainside and noticed how my mind was accumulating scientific data necessary for managing the forest, including information about different plant species, the health of those plants, and insect damage to the environment.

Exchanging Assumptions with Hypotheses

As I was thinking about the scientific data, I realized how dramatically my thought patterns had shifted since before I went to university. I remembered how as a young person I used to look up at a mountain and be awed by the beauty and grandeur of nature. Back then, I could have happily laid on a grass field or forest floor for hours. But years later, as I was working in the forest, I realized I could no longer see the beauty. I was shocked by how much my thought processes had been remolded.

I am not saying the change that took place in my brain was bad. It was just a different way of looking at nature. New neural pathways had been formed during my years at the university that caused me to see things scientifically rather than aesthetically. The new progressions of thought were helpful in managing the forest, but not helpful in allowing me to enjoy the beauty of nature.

I had two distinct neural pathways in my brain, each offering a specific perspective of the forest. Each pathway was like a program loaded into the computer of my brain. The first pathway formed when I was a young person. It selected and analyzed data from the forest, leading me to the conclusion that nature is awe-inspiring. The second pathway selected and analyzed the data, leading me to conclusions about how to manage the forest. I was able to use either program in my brain but to switch programs I had to stop, refocus, and look at the forest from a different perspective.

Point 3.26: My Progression Leading to Agnosticism

I had another progression of thought formed within my brain a few years later when I attended a seminary and worked on my Masters of Divinity degree. At seminary I spent month after month, analyzing other people's thoughts about God, religion, the Bible, the world, etc.

Has God Proven His Existence?

When I came out of the seminary, I experienced a period of disillusionment. I could read Greek, explain what Augustine had contributed to civilization, and outline the history of Christian thought, but I didn't know if God existed. Of course, not every student comes out of seminary as an agnostic, but I did.

Today, it has been over 40 years since I attended that seminary. I can still make my mind switch into that progression of thought leading to agnosticism but today I have other progressions that lead to theism. I have done the required work to form the necessary neural pathways. I have also worked to determine which pathway—the one leading to agnosticism or the one leading to theism—actually reveals truth.

Point 3.27: The Progression Blinding People from God

Students of Western philosophy must learn the progressions of thought that noted philosophers developed. They may have to learn the progression that led Plato to his conclusions, Aquinas to his conclusions, Bacon to his conclusions, Kant to his conclusions, and Nietzsche to his conclusions. Then those students will have to become so familiar with those progressions of thought that they will be required to prove their comprehension by writing papers and passing tests. When they merge those progressions of thought together, they will have formed the same neural pathways common to all students of Western philosophy.

As explained, the Western philosophical progression starts with the assumption of Plato's dualistic cosmology, then creates a greater and greater separation between God and the individual. Through that progression, God becomes difficult or impossible to see. That is similar to how I could not see the beauty of a forest after I finished my Bachelor of Science degree.

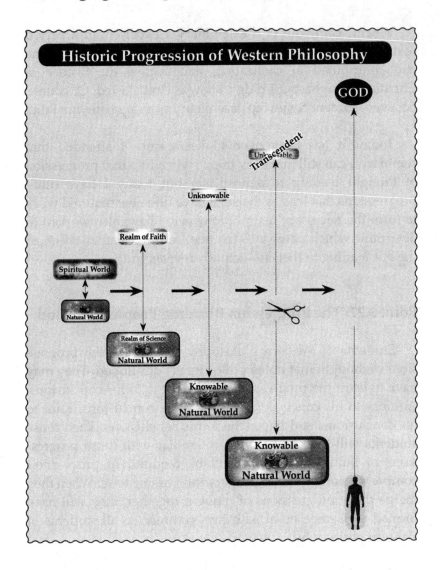

The student of Western philosophy will not only have a separation between the natural and spiritual worlds but also mounds of questions placed between themselves and God. Atheists like to propose questions like these:

"How can God exist since there is so much evil in the world?"

"Why do babies die if God loves humanity?"
"Why are people who claim to believe in God so bad?"
"What created God?"

These are devour questions. Let me explain.

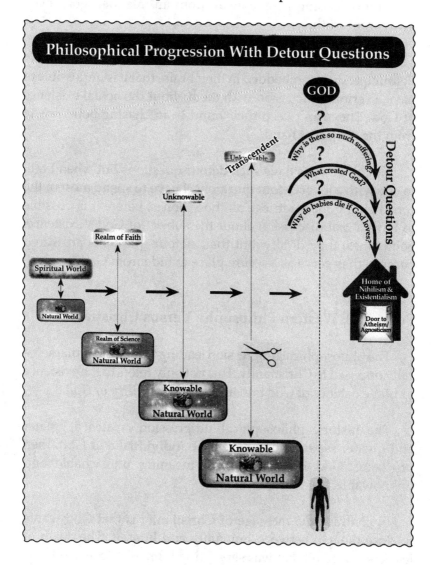

Exchanging Assumptions with Hypotheses

Each of the questions listed above deserves an answer, but in the midst of a discussion about the existence or non-existence of God, such questions are simply "detour questions." Remember, questions toss bones. Like dogs chase bones, people chase questions to their logical answer. Hence, questions can function as detours leading people away from an intended goal, even away from truth.

I have talked with some individuals who have so many detour questions embedded in their brain, that it is impossible to have a serious discussion with them about the actual existence of God. They can't keep their mind from chasing bones away from the subject at hand.

Not all atheists have such detour questions but when I talk to one with a lot of detour questions, I have to spend most of the time helping them retrieve all those bones, before it is possible to have a real discussion about the subject of God's existence. Sometimes, they don't want their detour questions answered because they serve as a secure place to hide from God.

Point 3.28: Western Philosophy Versus Christianity

The philosophical progression leading to atheism is diametrically opposed to Christianity. This not only refers to the existence or non-existence of God but also the *accessibility of God*.

The historic philosophical progression creates a greater and greater separation between the individual and God, then proclaims God is transcendent, meaning unreachable and unknowable.

In contrast, the message of Christianity is that God wants to close the gap between humanity and himself. The death of Jesus removed all that was separating humanity from God.

Within Christianity, there is a symbol often used to explain the accessibility of God. It is taken from a passage in the New Testament (Matthew 27:5) that reports how the veil in the temple in Jerusalem was torn in two exactly at the instant Jesus died on the cross. Before the veil in the temple was torn, it represented how God was separated from humanity. The instant the veil was torn represents how humanity can now go through the veil and have direct access to God.

Historic Western philosophy has been recreating that separation and trying sew the veil back together ever since.

Point 3.29: Are All People Biased?

We should not be surprised that the message of Western philosophy and the message of Christianity are diametrically opposed to each other.

It makes sense if we accept Hypothesis 2. If we accept that the heart is the control center of human nature, then we will understand why atheists have developed a progression of thought that leads to atheism and theists have developed a progression of the thought that leads to theism. Each has developed a progression of thought that leads where they wanted to go.

On the other hand, if we embrace the second assumption of Western philosophy that the intellect is the control center, then we will not recognize the biases seated in the heart of every person.

Unfortunately, people are usually quick to agree that their opponents are influenced by their biases, but they will not as readily agree that they themselves are equally influenced. I ask you to be consistent in applying Hypothesis 2 to yourself and to those who oppose you.

Exchanging Assumptions with Hypotheses

We are all influenced. The person who does not recognize this is naive. The person who thinks these dynamics are at work in their opponents' lives, but not their own, is blind.

Point 3.30: Everyone Thinks They Are Logical

Everyone thinks their own progression of thought is logical.

Of course, there are exceptions. A few people know they are insane, and a few others will admit they have trouble keeping their thoughts straight, but generally speaking, people see themselves as logical.

Some people are convinced they are logical and everyone else is illogical. I listened to one philosophy professor so convinced his progression of thought was the only logical progression that he felt obligated to uproot any contrary ways of thinking among his students. He regularly ridiculed any student who expressed contrary ideas. He viciously attacked and publicly humiliated anyone who dared question his views. He would not tolerate other progressions of thought contrary to the historic Western philosophical progression of thought.

In reality, that progression is just another way of thinking. Admittedly, the historical philosophical progression has had some brilliant people working on it during the last 2,400 years. It is fine-tuned. The answers given are very logical but the questions are biased. It is essential to realize the historical philosophical progression is just *a* progression of thought. It is not *the* logical progression.

Consider how tens of thousands of people have changed from theism to atheism and tens of thousands have changed from atheism to theism.[36] The person who converts one way or the other is just as smart before they convert as they are after they convert. This reveals an important truth. Sometimes people think their opponents are irrational and ignorant, but that can't be correct since the same person who is an atheist at one point will be a theist at another point. Therefore, differences cannot be the result of the people on one side being irrational or ignorant.

There are intelligent people on both sides, and as stated, everyone's progression of thought seems logical to them.

Point 3.31: Check the Assumptions at the Foundation

Because atheists think their progression of thought is logical and theists think their progression of thought is logical, it is illogical to choose what progression of thought is true based on whether or not it seems logical. Of course, we do not want to embrace a progression of thought that is obviously irrational, requiring huge blind leaps, but when there are smart people claiming each progression is logical, we must look to some other feature of a thought progression to determine if it is true.

So what should we examine before we decide which progression is true?

1. Examine the assumptions at the foundation of those progressions
2. Examine the heart of those who developed those progressions
3. Examine the supporting evidence

---

36 Many studies have been carried out to determine the demographics of atheism, but results are spread widely in both the increasing and decreasing directions mostly because of how difficult it is to define words like atheist or agnostic.

Exchanging Assumptions with Hypotheses

Section 5 of this book is dedicated to examining *the evidence for atheism versus theism.* So, we will not deal with point number 3 listed above until Section 5. In the remaining pages here in Section 3, look with me at the *assumptions* and *heart.*

We identified two assumptions upon which Western philosophy has been built.

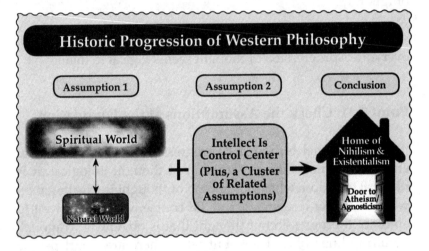

We also identified two hypotheses as alternatives to the assumptions of Western philosophy.

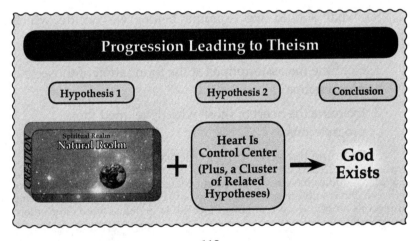

With reference to the two cosmologies, I have come to believe Paul's cosmology (the biblically-derived cosmology) more accurately explains reality than Plato's cosmology. I hope you will continue to test it as a hypothesis and decide for yourself.

Concerning the second assumption (that the intellect is the control center) and its alternative hypothesis (that the heart is the control center), I do not believe it is a difficult exchange. Given any serious thought, I think reasonable people will admit that the heart does influence the intellect.

Of course, some readers may want to qualify their understanding of the human heart. They may agree that desires, affections, love, faith, and hope influence thought patterns, but some readers may not agree that these are functions of the heart. They may identify these as functions of the intellect or some other part of human nature. As a result, those readers may want to qualify their agreement with Hypothesis 2, by assigning the identified functions to something other than the heart. I respect that viewpoint.

Even though I respect that viewpoint, I will continue referring to the heart and I will be thinking of it as the seat of desires, affections, love, faith, and hope. If you can respect my viewpoint, we will be able to finish our discussion on this.

Point 3.32: The Heart of Affection, Admiration, and Love

In order to determine if a progression of thought is true, we should not only look at the assumptions lying at its foundation but also at the heart of those who developed and hold to that progression.

Exchanging Assumptions with Hypotheses

Consider the influence of affections, admiration, and love. The thoughts of people tend to conform to the thoughts of individuals whom they admire. Leaders in the advertising industry have been taking advantage of this for years, repeatedly showing admired people using the products that the advertiser wants to promote. We all have a tendency to bring our thoughts into alignment with people we look up to and/or love. Therefore, it is just natural to let our thoughts conform to our parents, teachers, heroes, and others whom we respect and admire.

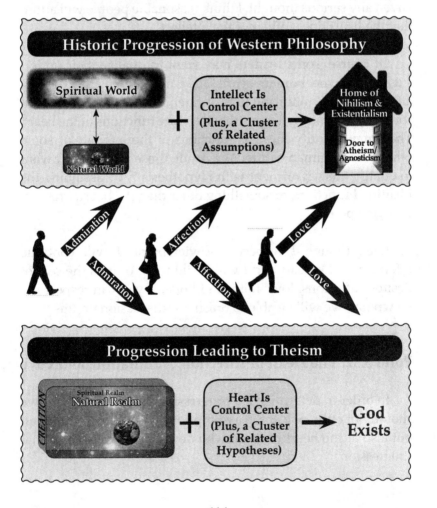

There are also opposing influences, such as when a young person makes a choice diametrically opposed to their parents. Such a choice may seem very logical to the young person, but the choice may actually be determined by the young person's desire to break free from or even hurt their parents.

Because our thoughts are influenced by those with whom we have a relationship, changing one way of thinking for another way of thinking is often an emotional experience. In the process of change, people sometimes feel like they are betraying the person who taught them their initial way of thinking. They don't want to abandon their previously held view because of their admiration and love for the person who taught them that view.

Sometimes thought patterns are influenced by an entire group of relationships. For this reason, an individual may feel she is being disloyal to an entire group when even considering a contrary way of thinking.

Such influences on the thoughts of people are real. When considering why people think the way they think, it is not enough to follow their progression of thought and see if it is logical. We must consider the thoughts of people to whom they are committed, admire, and love.

Point 3.33: Look at the Heart for Anger

Other features of the heart that influence thoughts are hate, unforgiveness, and anger. Knowing this, I am skeptical about what is said by:

- A husband talking about his unfaithful wife, or vice versa

Exchanging Assumptions with Hypotheses

- A neo-nazi talking about Jews
- A political activist speaking about a president elected from the opposing party
- A teenager who has been kicked out of school explaining the lack of fairness of the principal
- A conspiracy theorist talking about the government
- A Muslim terrorist describing an infidel
- Me when I am mad

It does not matter how logical people think they are, hate, unforgiveness, and anger do influence their thoughts.

Now consider the anger issues many atheists have revealed. The popular atheist activist Greta Christina admitted to the journalist Chris Mooney on the *Point of Inquiry* podcast, "there isn't one emotion" that affects atheists "but anger is one of the emotions that many of us have ...[it] drives others to participate in the movement."[37]

Among leading atheists, hate toward and disappointment with their father is especially evident. Sigmund Freud despised his Jewish father and wrote that his father was a sexual pervert. One of the most famous atheists, Bertrand Russell, lost his father when he was four years old; then Bertrand was raised by his rigidly puritanical grandmother, who was known as "Deadly Nightshade." Friedrich Nietzche, who is known for his declaration that "God is dead!", lost his father (who was a pastor) before his fifth birthday. The famous atheist, David Hume, was two years old when he lost his father. Jean-Paul Sartre was fifteen months old when he lost his father. The most known leader of the French Enlightenment, Arouet, hated his father so much that he changed his name to Voltaire. Voltaire's father was so angry with his son

---

37 Greta Christina, *Why Are You Atheists So Angry?*

116

that at one point he made arrangements to have his son sent into prison or exile.[38] [39]

It is no secret that the most noted philosophical leaders of the Enlightenment were angry at established religion. For some, it was their constant drumbeat, and they became famous for writing aggressive condemnations of the Christian Church.

I heard one man who claimed to be an atheist talk about his hate for God. Of course, that in itself is a contradiction in thought. He described how years earlier when he was a soldier, he used to take his machine gun and shoot up into the air shouting profanities at God. He blamed God for many horrendous things that happened to him as a child.

I don't mean to imply that every atheist is angry. Most of the masses in atheistic communist countries simply accepted what they were taught. Most of the children raised in atheistic homes learned and embraced the views of their parents. Many students at universities became atheists because they could not counter the logic of the arguments presented to them by their professors. Those atheists are probably not motivated by anger, but many of the vocal atheists who laid the fundamental thought patterns of atheism have definitely displayed an abnormal amount of anger.

Point 3.34: Look at the Heart for Hidden Motives

Anger does influence people but so also do other motivating factors. Some of them are hidden.

---

38 This information about atheists and their relationships to their father has been taken from: https://probe.org/atheists-and-their-fathers/ Retrieved April 2019. More information about this can be found in Paul Vitz's book, *Faith of the Fatherless*.

39 Voltaire devoted much of his life criticizing religion, and especially Christianity, but he was not an atheist. Voltaire was a deist, believing in an impersonal God.

Exchanging Assumptions with Hypotheses

Detectives often "follow the money" when trying to solve a criminal case. Why? Because whoever expects to end up with the money has a strong motivation to commit the related crime. Sometimes the motive has nothing to do with money. If the detective can identify some other motive, they are well on their way to identifying who did it.

Consider atheism. Are there any hidden motives or benefits to becoming an atheist?

In Section 2, we discussed how atheists say they are free of moral absolutes. Free from guilt/shame. Free from rules corresponding to religious, cultural, and familial values. And free to do whatever they desire. Atheists have been proclaiming this freedom as good news for many years.

Sexual desires are some of the strongest desires people experience. Those desires pull people into corresponding behaviors and then they have to deal with the consequences, including the guilt/shame induced by previously held values. Living with guilt/shame is difficult. Guilt/shame can cause pain like physical sickness can cause pain. People who are sick and in pain search for a cure. So also, people suffering under guilt/shame search for a cure. Atheism offers an escape.

I don't mean to say or imply that everyone who is an atheist became an atheist to rationalize their sexual behavior or to escape guilt/shame. However, it seems more than coincidence that most people who become atheists outside of atheistic societies, do so between ages 16 and 28 when their sexual desires are most powerful and they are first separated from their family relationships that tie them to previously held values. Raging hormones throw many people into a crisis of values. Trying to understand what is going on can be extremely difficult. While grasping for understanding, atheism offers one solution.

Therefore, we should consider it as one factor influencing some people to embrace the atheistic progression of thought.

For theism, the very opposite influence is at work. A person who becomes a theist is well aware of the implication that part of the package is to govern one's life according to the morals and values of the God in whom one believes.

Hence, there is a cost to being a theist. That same cost is not inherent with atheism. Recognizing that absence of cost, we should consider the possibility that some people choose to be an atheist simply because they don't want to live according to the dictates of God.

Point 3.35: Look at the Heart for Pride

Finally, we should consider how pride in the heart can influences thought patterns.

We already explained (point 2.12) how the world of atheism offers a throne. It offers an elevated place to sit from where atheists can see why they do not have to submit to traditional, religious, or familial rules. Atheism calls for a posture of life that refuses to bow to any being outside of oneself. It claims an identity for oneself as one of the enlightened ones surrounded by the weak, naive masses who are enslaved puppets being manipulated by society and especially the religious elite. Since there is no god, the individual must govern themselves and trust in themselves.

Of course, there is a certain positive outcome when a person is self-confident. In contrast to the person who is filled with self-doubt and insecurities, the self-assured person is able to face challenges and accomplish much.

Exchanging Assumptions with Hypotheses

However, there is also a point at which self-confidence crosses over into pride that distorts one's thought patterns. The individual deceived by pride is not usually aware of their own deception. Deception by definition means the individual does not know they are deceived. Yet, observant onlookers can more easily identify it.

Let me explain the deceptive influence of pride by talking about its recognized role in the life of the alcoholic. Here, I do not mean to associate atheism with alcoholism but I want to identify how pride does influence thought patterns.

Modern alcohol treatment programs are designed to confront specific progressions of thought that are common to most alcoholics. Those progressions have been clearly identified by professionals in the field and are aggressively challenged in treatment programs.

Millions of alcoholics have been helped by a program known as *Alcoholics Anonymous*. In that program, alcoholics are helped through 12 steps to recovery and all of those steps are founded on the idea that the person must bow to a higher power. It is not necessary to identify who or what that higher power is, but the posture of humility is recognized as necessary to "restore us to sanity."[40] Indeed, there is something about bowing that is necessary to break the progression of thought common in the alcoholic's mind.

Having been around alcoholics for most of my life and having been through an alcoholic treatment program as a family member of an alcoholic, I can tell you that alcoholics who find freedom from their addiction commonly display characteristics of brokenness and humility. This is in contrast to alcoholics

---

40 Taken from the second step in the *Alcoholics Anonymous 12 Step Recovery Program*.

who never do get free but who cling to a specific progression of thought and along with it a posture that they do not have to bow to any higher power.

Some readers may question what this has to do with atheism. Pride lends itself to distorted progressions of thought. In my experience with atheists, I have seen a shared arrogance and posture of pride that sends up red flags. It is another reason I am skeptical of the atheistic progression of thought.

Point 3.36: Decisions Come from a Desire of the Heart

Finally, we should look at the actual decision to become an atheist. Of course, millions have become atheists because they were raised in an atheistic community or home. They simply conformed to the people in their immediate world. As a result, many of them never actually made a conscious decision to become an atheist.

But the rest who made a decision had to have had some reason.

As we discussed in point 1.17, Western philosophy can only lead someone to the front door of atheism/agnosticism. There is no logical progression of thought that leads a person to become an atheist/agnostic. Each student of philosophy must make a personal decision whether or not to step across the threshold. Atheism/agnosticism is a choice.

Why would someone make that choice? As we have been discussing, the heart, not the intellect, is the ultimate control center of a person's being. With the heart as the seat of desire, the person who makes a decision to be an atheist/agnostic must *want* to be an atheist/agnostic. There must be something they desire that the atheistic/agnostic lifestyle offers.

Exchanging Assumptions with Hypotheses

What could that be? The desire of their heart may correspond with any of the heart motivations we have mentioned: affection, admiration, or love of others who are atheists / agnostics; hate, unforgiveness, or anger; freedom from guilt/shame and rules associated with religious values; or pride. People may also choose to be an atheist/agnostic because they desire to rule their own life and refuse to bow to any higher authority such as god.

For some people, being an atheist may not be a direct choice, but rather the avoidance of a choice. They don't want to deal with the implications of God's existence. They know that admitting God exists means they will have to readjust their lifestyle. They will have to reconsider why certain tragic events happened in their life. Rethinking the related issues can be too painful or difficult to deal with at the present time. It is just easier to continue living independently of God.

Of course, there could be other reasons that we have not identified here, but building on Hypothesis 2, that the heart is the control center of human nature, leads us to conclude that what is in the heart is more determinative than what is in the intellect in decision-making, and that includes the decision to be an atheist or a theist.

If, indeed, the heart is more determinative than the intellect, then changing from an atheist to a theist or changing from a theist to an atheist requires a change in heart. An intellectual argument—no matter how logical it is—will not be enough. If the heart is the control center of human nature, then a change in heart will be required.

Summary of Section Three

We examined two progressions of thought, the Western philosophical progression leading to atheism / agnosticism and a second progression of thought leading to theism.

We identified two assumptions upon which Western philosophy is built:

1. Plato's dualistic cosmology:
    a. with the spiritual and natural worlds separate
    b. with God isolated from the natural world

2. The intellect is the control center of a person's being

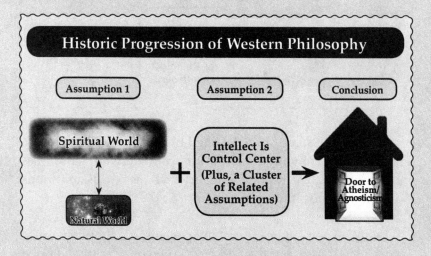

Exchanging Assumptions with Hypotheses

As explained in the text, the concepts identified above are referred to as *assumptions* because students sitting in philosophically-influenced classrooms are never encouraged to test these assumptions. Yet, these two assumptions lie at the foundation of almost all philosophical discussions.

In this section, we asked you to replace the two assumptions of Western philosophy with two biblically-derived hypotheses:

1. A cosmology with the spiritual and natural realms filling the same space and integrated
2. The heart is the control center of a person's being

We encourage you to treat these concepts as hypotheses and test them for yourself.

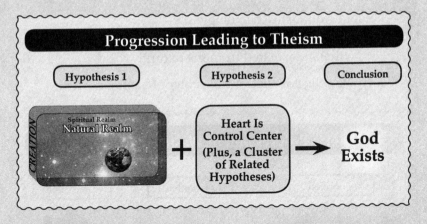

I explained some of the testing I have done and, as a result, I have become convinced that the biblically-derived hypotheses more accurately correspond to reality than the two assumptions of Western philosophy.

I don't expect you to accept my conclusions simply because I have stated them, but they deserve your consideration. I hope you will investigate and test to your own satisfaction.

If you build on these two hypotheses, a progression of thought will develop that leads to theism. In contrast, a progression of thought built on the two assumptions of Western philosophy will lead to atheism / agnosticism.

These two conclusions—theism or atheism / agnosticism—are not predetermined or inescapable. It depends partly upon the individuals who are building the progressions. We all like to think we are logical, but we have different ways of putting thoughts together which may lead us to different conclusions. However, generally speaking, people who follow the progression built upon the assumptions of Western philosophy will arrive at atheism / agnosticism. Generally speaking, people who build upon the biblically-derived hypotheses will arrive at theism.

Everyone's progression of thought seems logical to themselves. For this reason, we not only examined the assumptions / hypotheses of the two views, but we also considered the heart issues motivating individuals. We looked at key heart issues that may raise red flags for you. They certainly do for me when investigating the atheistic progression of thought.

What remains for us to do now is decide which progression is true. With that goal before us, we will develop an accurate understanding of faith in Section 4, then discuss the evidence / proof for God's existence in Section 5.

What Is Faith?

Before we examine the evidence/proof for the existence of God, we must have an accurate understanding of faith. This will become very clear as we contrast the philosophically-derived understanding of faith with the biblically-derived understanding of faith.

Point 4.1: Faith Is a Function of the Heart

Our beginning assumptions determine much about our final conclusion and also about the definitions of many keywords along the way to the conclusion. Let's see how our assumptions influence our definition of "faith."

Since the Western mind tends to see the intellect as the control center of a person's being, Western people, at least those trained in Western philosophy, think of faith as a function of the intellect. This is reinforced by Plato's cosmology which is seated deeply at the foundation of Western civilization. Especially formative is Plato's assumption that the intellect gives people access to the spiritual world and all truth.

PLATO:
PEOPLE ACCESS THE SPIRITUAL WORLD THROUGH THEIR THOUGHTS

During the Scientific Revolution, the separation between the spiritual world and the natural world became greater and greater. Then faith was assigned to the spiritual world

What Is Faith?

and knowledge was assigned to the natural world. As faith and knowledge were separated, faith and knowledge were contrasted. With that contrast, faith became understood as *the acceptance of ideas without evidence.* Soon after, faith became understood as the *acceptance of the unknowable and unprovable.*

Notice how this philosophical understanding of faith revolves around the acceptance of certain *thoughts* and the absence of *reasoning.* These thoughts and reasonings are associated with functions of the intellect. This corresponds with the Western assumption that the intellect is the control center of a person's being.

In contrast, if we start with the biblically-derived hypotheses that we identified in Section 3, we will understand that the heart guides the intellect and the heart is the seat of desires, affections, love, faith, and hope (explained in points 3.10-3.12).

As we now go on to discuss faith from the biblical perspective, we will talk simultaneously about both the noun, "faith," and the corresponding verb, "believe." Paul wrote:

> . . . *for with the heart a person believes . . .*
> Romans 10:10

To fully understand the heart as the seat of faith and believing, we must abandon the cosmology of Western philosophy. Instead, we must build on the biblically-derived cosmology. Therefore, we will envision a world in which the spiritual and natural realms are integrated. Corresponding to this, we will see human nature as existing in both the spiritual and natural realms. The spiritual soul is integrated with the physical body (explained in points 3.11-3.12). As a result, the heart exists in both the spiritual and natural realms. It is that integrated heart that is the seat of faith and belief.

BIBLICALLY-DERIVED UNDERSTANDING:
COSMOLOGY WITH SPIRITUAL AND NATURAL REALMS INTEGRATED;
SPIRITUAL SOUL INTEGRATED WITH PHYSICAL BODY;
FAITH AS A FUNCTION OF THE HEART

So according to the biblically-derived understanding, faith is a function of the heart, not the intellect.

Point 4.2: Biblical Understanding: Faith Is Trust

Next, it is important to know that people in the Bible thought in *relational terminology*, in comparison to modern English-speaking people who think primarily in *abstract terminology*. Relational words have meaning derived from identifying associations. Abstract words have a definition which isolates and distinguishes the meaning from all other words.

To see this distinction, consider how a Jewish rabbi, who thinks in relational terms, may introduce the Jewish Scriptures to a group of students. He may do it by carefully placing a drop of honey on the Scriptures in front of each student, then saying to the student, "Lick the honey, and know from this day forward what the Scriptures are like." An association is made.

What Is Faith?

In contrast, a teacher who thinks in abstract terms like most English-speakers is likely to introduce the Scriptures to students by explaining how the Scriptures differ from all other written materials.

Some modern cultures think relationally like the Jews in the Bible did, while other modern cultures, including most Western people, tend to think in abstract terms. As a result, Western people, who think in abstract terms and assume the intellect is the control center of human nature, will tend to define faith as *a mental assent to certain ideas.*

In contrast, most of the people in the Bible would have understood the word "faith" to be a synonym for "trust." Trust is a relational word. Trust carries the connotation of one person depending upon another. So also, faith—when understood in its biblical context—carries a connotation of one person depending upon another. When used in the context of faith in God, they would have thought of trust in God.

UNDERSTANDING OF FAITH

Western Philosophical	Biblically-derived
1. A function of the intellect	1. A function of the heart
2. Mental assent to ideas	2. Trust

Point 4.3: The Relationship of Faith With Evidence

As we continue developing our understanding of faith, we can now identify its relationship with *evidence*.

In Section 1, we traced the historic Western philosophical progression and saw how faith was assigned to the spiritual world and contrasted with knowledge. So faith and knowledge were separated, even set up as opposing concepts.

WESTERN PHILOSOPHY:
FAITH ASSIGNED TO SPIRITUAL WORLD
AND CONTRASTED WITH KNOWLEDGE

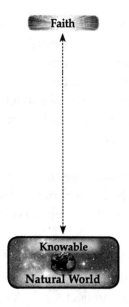

That separation between faith and knowledge became more fixed in Western philosophy, as teachers like Soren Kierkegaard argued that religious faith is always *irrational* since it requires *a blind leap*. During that period, faith became understood as *mental assent to certain ideas without evidence.*

As already mentioned, some philosophers antagonistic to religion went even further, saying faith is "the great cop-out," "the excuse to evade the need to think," and the "vice of any religion."[41] For some, faith is an evil that is still stubbornly persisting in society.

In contrast, those who wrote the Bible held an understanding of "faith" that was very different. To see this, we must

---

41 Cited in Francis Collins. *The Language of God* (NY: Free Press. 2006), pt. 4.

What Is Faith?

first realize *faith is always built on evidence. Faith is never a blind leap.* Faith, as understood in the Bible, is always a rational step.

This truth is difficult for those trained in Western philosophy to accept because a major feature of their progression of thought is their definition of faith. Along their 2,400-year-long progression, they settled on a definition of faith as the mental assent to ideas without evidence. That definition is an anchor for Western philosophy. For someone to challenge that definition is to challenge their entire progression of thought.

Yet, that is exactly what we must do. When discussing the subject of evidence, the biblical definition of faith is the polar opposite of the Western philosophical definition.

UNDERSTANDING OF FAITH

Western Philosophical	Biblically-derived
1. A function of the intellect	1. A function of the heart
2. Mental assent to ideas	2. Trust
3. Irrational step	**3. Rational step**
4. Blind leap	

Have you ever tried to have a discussion with a person who has very different definitions of key words that you are trying to use? It is very difficult. This is precisely the problem in discussions between atheists / agnostics and theists. In particular, theists who embrace a biblically-derived understanding of faith see faith as always built upon evidence.

To see this, let's consider the biblically-derived understanding concerning how faith is produced. Let me show you how faith in the Bible is built on evidence, and it requires both the intellect and the heart.

Point 4.4: Faith Comes by Hearing

The word "faith" can be used in many different contexts. For example, we can talk about having faith that our food is not poisonous. In this book, we are not talking about that kind of faith. As we talk about the biblically-derived understanding of faith, we are talking about faith in God. As we talk about the Christian understanding of faith, we are also talking about faith in Jesus.

In the Bible, Paul wrote:

> *So faith comes from hearing, and hearing by the word of Christ.*
>
> Romans 10:17

According to this, people must hear the "word of Christ."

During the first century when this Bible verse was written, the "word of Christ" referred to words that reveal who Jesus Christ is. Those words could have been words spoken by Jesus or words spoken by other people that reveal who Jesus is. The words of other people would have included other people's witness and testimonies about what Jesus said and did. According to the verse quoted above, faith comes as a result of hearing from Jesus or testimonies about Jesus.

As we consider this, it does not matter whether you personally accept or don't accept what the Bible reports about Jesus. What we are looking at here is the *definition of faith according to those who wrote the Bible*. They understood that hearing the word of Christ precedes faith.

For an example of this understanding of faith, consider the

What Is Faith?

biblical report of a woman who talked with Jesus and then told everyone in her city about him. After she did, the Bible reports that, "From that city many . . . believed in him because of the word of the woman who testified . . . " (John 4:39). Notice her testimony about Jesus preceded the people's faith in Jesus. Afterwards, Jesus stayed in that city for a time and talked with all the people. Later, they said to the woman, "It is no longer because of what you said that we believe, for we have heard for ourselves . . ." (John 4:42). So, first they believed because of the testimony of the woman, but later they believed because they heard from Jesus himself.

Hearing precedes faith.

To the people in Bible times, the *witness and testimonies* that other people speak were *evidence*. People have to hear the evidence before they believe.

BIBLICALLY-DERIVED UNDERSTANDING: FAITH COMES FROM HEARING EVIDENCE

But no adult accepts the testimonies of others unless they consider the source of those testimonies is credible. Evaluation of testimonies requires logical thought. Evaluation is a function of the intellect. A person must hear the testimonies, then evaluate the reliability of the source.

A good example of this is how throngs of people are reported in the Bible as following Jesus. They heard reports of what he was doing, and so, they sought him out. The people who followed Jesus must have assigned some credibility to the testimonies they heard about Jesus. Otherwise, they never would have sought him.

So hearing testimonies (which is evidence) comes first, then evaluation of the credibility of the evidence, and then faith is produced. The evaluation is a function of the intellect, but faith is a function of the heart.

We cannot emphasize this enough: faith is a change in heart that happens after evidence has been heard, then evaluated and determined to be credible.

Of course, this is very different than the philosophically-derived understanding of faith which recognizes no evidence for faith. Because of that difference we need to clearly establish that this is the biblical understanding of faith.

Point 4.5: Faith Comes by Reading

In order to produce faith in the heart, testimonies about Jesus do not have to be spoken. They can also be written. John explained how he wrote down many of the miracles of Jesus, "so that you may believe that Jesus is the Christ, the Son of God" (John 20:31). Indeed, many people come to believe in Jesus as a result of reading what other people have written about him. So faith, according to the Bible writers, comes as a result of hearing and / or reading about Jesus.

What Is Faith?

Again, the credibility of the evidence must be evaluated by the intellect, but faith is a change in heart that follows.

BIBLICALLY-DERIVED UNDERSTANDING:
FAITH COMES FROM HEARING AND READING

Point 4.6: Faith Comes by Seeing and Experiencing

Faith is not only the product of hearing and reading but also *seeing*. There are several verses in the Bible that make this association between seeing and believing.[42]

Consider the biblical reports of Jesus' first appearance to his apostles after his death and resurrection. We are told Jesus appeared to his apostles[43] and the apostles were made believers. So in that case, *seeing* Jesus alive resulted in faith.

Again, it does not matter whether you personally accept the Bible's reports of miracles. What we are doing it trying to understand how those who wrote the Bible understood faith. Those Bible writers understood that people must hear, read, or see evidence, before faith results.

42 E.g., Exodus 4:1-9; Numbers 14:11; John 10:38; 20:27.
43 John 20:19-20.

Each example of people seeing and then believing could also be explained as people *experiencing* and then believing.

Consider the Bible's account of how Paul was persecuting Christians, even having them put to death. The Bible reports that Jesus revealed himself to Paul in a blinding light, knocking Paul off his donkey and speaking from heaven (Acts 9:1-6). That experience turned Paul's life around, and as a result, he spent the rest of his days telling people about Jesus. Paul's dramatic experience made him a believer.

The Bible also reports about a man born blind experiencing a miracle of receiving sight. After the miracle, Jesus asked the healed man, "Do you believe in the Son of Man?" (John 9:35). The man answered, "Lord, I believe" (John 9:38). As a result of experiencing the miracle, the man believed.

So then, for faith to be produced in the heart, a person must hear, read, see, and / or experience.

Biblically-Derived Understanding: Faith Comes from Hearing, Reading, Seeing, and Experiencing

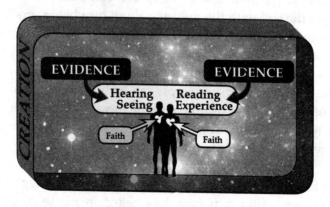

What Is Faith?

Point 4.7: Faith Is a Step Beyond Intellectual Evaluation

As we have explained, the biblically-derived understanding of faith involves the intellect and the heart. The intellect is necessary for the evaluation of whatever is heard, read, seen, and/or experienced. A person must evaluate the evidence and make a rational decision. Then a heart change must take place.

Faith (trust) is a step beyond the evaluation of the evidence. For this reason, some people may accumulate enough evidence to be intellectually convinced of some reality, but still not have a corresponding change in heart.

For an example of faith placed in a natural entity, consider an individual who learns that a certain bank is dependable, then decides to place their money in that bank. It would be possible that a certain person determines that a bank is dependable, but chooses not to trust that bank. Trust is a yielding, a commitment, a decision to rely upon that which has been determined to be true.

Jesus used several parables to explain how faith grows in the heart (e.g., Matthew 13:1-23). He compared seeds being cast into the soil with the message about him being proclaimed throughout the world. Then Jesus compared the soil where the seeds landed with the hearts of humanity. He said some soil is hard, some is rocky, some is filled with weeds, and some is good soil. So also, the hearts of people can be hard, consumed in the cares of the world, or receptive to the message about Jesus. The seeds will only grow in good soil. So also, the message about Jesus will only take root in people with a willing heart.

So faith, according to the Bible writers, is a change in heart that happens after a person has heard, read, seen, and/or experienced and then evaluated the evidence.

Point 4.8: Clearing Up Confusion About Faith

The philosophically-derived understanding of faith is fundamentally different than the biblically-derived understanding. Atheists, who commonly accept the philosophical understanding of faith, tend to see faith as a blind leap only taken by irrational, gullible people who lack something in their character, and therefore, need a crutch on which to lean. In contrast, those who embrace the biblically-derived understanding of faith recognize faith as a change in heart that takes place after a person has gathered and evaluated evidence with their intellect.

Understanding of Faith

Western Philosophical	Biblically-derived
1. A function of the intellect	1. A function of the heart
2. Mental assent to ideas	2. Trust
3. Irrational	3. Rational
4. Blind leap	4. Produced by: hearing, reading, seeing, experiencing
5. No evidence	5. Based on evidence
6. No association with heart	6. Change in heart

Point 4.9: Soren Kierkegaard's Mistake

As explained earlier, Soren Kierkegaard played a key role in developing the Western philosophical understanding of faith. But Soren used the Bible to support it. How was that possible?

Soren used the Bible, but he arrived at the philosophical understanding because he built on Plato's dualistic cosmology,

What Is Faith?

the assumption that the intellect is the control center of human nature, and Kant's total separation of the spiritual and natural worlds. Soren also used two carefully selected passages from the Bible. When only certain Bible passages are selected as Soren did, the meaning of those passages is easy to misunderstand or be purposely twisted to mean something that the original writers did not intend. Let me explain.

THE DEVELOPMENT OF SOREN KIERKEGAARD'S (MIS)UNDERSTANDING OF FAITH

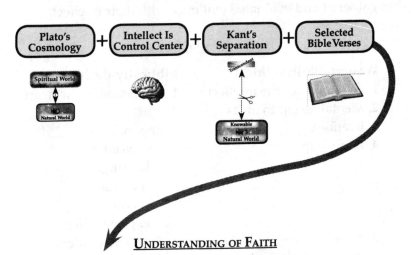

UNDERSTANDING OF FAITH

Western Philosophical
1. A function of the intellect
2. Mental assent to ideas
3. Irrational
4. Blind leap

Biblically-derived
1. A function of the heart
2. Trust
3. Rational
4. Produced by:
   hearing,
   reading,
   seeing,
   experiencing

5. No evidence
6. No association with heart

5. Based on evidence
6. Change in heart

In his book *Fear and Trembling*, Soren took a story from the Bible about a time God told Abraham to kill his own son and sacrifice that son.[44] Soren interpreted that story to mean that God required Abraham to take a leap of faith, in the sense of doing something which is totally irrational.

In reality, Soren missed the primary lesson of Abraham offering his son to God. Abraham had walked with God for many years. Of course, atheists cannot accept this because they do not believe anyone can walk with God. But here, we are trying to identify the definition of faith according to those who wrote the Bible.

Soren misunderstood. He thought people must first have faith, then take a blind leap, then God will reveal himself.

Soren Kierkegaard's Misunderstanding of Faith

Contrary to Soren's understanding, what actually happened in the Bible's report of Abraham's life is God revealed himself to Abraham over the course of many years, sometimes speaking audibly and even appearing in human form to Abraham. That resulted in faith, and because Abraham had faith (trust), he stepped forward to take a rational step of obedience.

Biblically-Derived Understanding of Faith

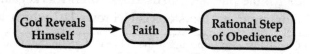

---

44 You can read the story in Genesis 22:1-19.

What Is Faith?

This biblically-derived understanding recognizes that God's revelation of himself precedes faith. Faith comes as a result of hearing, reading, seeing, or experiencing. Evidence comes first, then faith follows.

Nowhere in the Bible is there any example of God asking someone to believe without first having evidence.

In the biblical report of Jesus' first appearance to his apostles after he rose from the dead, Thomas was not with them. Later, Jesus appeared to Thomas and said to him:

> *Reach here with your finger, and see My hands; and reach here your hand and put it into My side; and do not be unbelieving, but believing.*
>
> John 20:27

Jesus allowed Thomas to touch and see him. After Thomas did, he believed, saying, "My Lord and my God!" (John 20:28). Talk about hands-on evidence!

Not all people get first-hand evidence of God, because God also expected people to believe in him when they heard or read about him. Yet, God always provided first or second-hand evidence (meaning evidence that is spoken or written by someone else) before expecting people to believe.[45]

Point 4.10: Another Misunderstanding of Soren

Another Bible passage misused by Soren Kierkegaard and others following in his footsteps is Hebrews 11:1 which says:

---

45 Some Christians who build upon the Bible will argue that God always provides firsthand evidence. They can say this, because they consider secondhand evidence only the starting point for faith. They will explain God always reveals himself personally to the individual after they begin to open their heart.

Has God Proven His Existence?

Now faith is the assurance of things hoped for,
the conviction of things not seen.

People who wrongly use this verse to teach the philosophical understanding of faith like to focus on the last three words, "things not seen." Then they explain how faith is to do something which cannot be seen in the sense of it "cannot be understood." In other words, they equate "things not seen" with "doing the irrational."

Soren Kierkegaard's Misunderstanding of Hebrews 11:1:

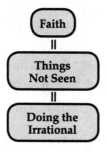

That is a profound misunderstanding of what Hebrews 11:1 says. Admittedly, someone reading the Bible through the lens of Western philosophy (Plato's cosmology, the intellect being the control center, plus Kant's separation, plus Soren's blind leap) may come to that understanding, but the writer of Hebrews had a biblical cosmology and a biblically-derived understanding of human nature. His worldview led him to understand faith differently than a modern philosophically-trained person.

The writer of Hebrews 11:1 first defined faith as the "conviction" and the "assurance." In Hebrews 11:1, the writer aligned these as synonyms.

What Is Faith?

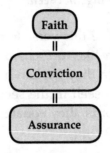

Abraham had a conviction and assurance in his heart because he knew God. That is what the writer of Hebrews was explaining. Faith is conviction, assurance, confidence, and trust!

The writer also aligned "things hoped for" and "things not seen." The things "hoped for" referred to the same things as those "not seen."

BIBLICALLY-DERIVED UNDERSTANDING OF HEBREWS 11:1:

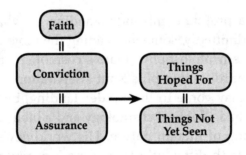

The writer of Hebrews was *not* talking about things that are irrational. He was talking about things not seen in the present, but will become true in the future—"things hoped for." In other words, faith is the conviction, assurance, confidence, and trust that the things hoped for will come true even though they cannot be seen with the eyes at the present time.

BIBLICALLY-DERIVED UNDERSTANDING OF HEBREWS 11:1:

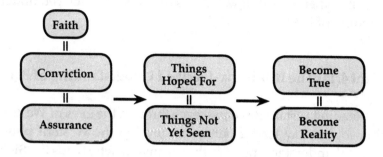

This understanding is confirmed when we read more in the Bible about Abraham's faith. Before preparing his son for the sacrifice, Abraham confidently stated, "God will provide for Himself the lamb for the burnt offering . . ." (Genesis 22:8). Abraham expressed his faith (confidence and assurance) that God would intervene. Hebrews 11:19 explains how Abraham had faith that God may even raise Isaac from the dead. Abraham was not taking a blind leap. He was acting based on his years of experience walking with God. Abraham expressed his faith by saying God will provide a lamb or even raise Isaac from the dead if necessary.

BIBLICALLY-DERIVED UNDERSTANDING:
FAITH IS CONVICTION AND ASSURANCE

What Is Faith?

Of course, atheists cannot incorporate this understanding of faith into their worldview, but it is the biblically-derived understanding of faith.

Point 4.11: The Biblically-Derived Understanding of Faith

Reading certain Bible passages through the eyes of Western philosophy may lead a person to develop the Western philosophical understanding of faith, but anyone who reads the Bible with the biblically-derived cosmology and the understanding that the heart is the control center of human nature will develop the biblical understanding of faith.

BIBLICALLY-DERIVED UNDERSTANDING OF FAITH

UNDERSTANDING OF FAITH

Western Philosophical	Biblically-derived
1. A function of the intellect	1. A function of the heart
2. Mental assent to ideas	2. Trust
3. Irrational	3. Rational
4. Blind leap	4. Produced by: hearing, reading, seeing, experiencing
5. No evidence	5. Based on evidence
6. No association with heart	6. Change in heart

Has God Proven His Existence?

Because the definitions of faith are so extremely different, I will put the word **"faith"** in bold letters when using the biblically-derived definition in the remaining pages of this book.

Point 4.12: Most of What We Believe Has Been Taught to Us

Remember that **faith** recognizes evidence that comes through hearing, reading, seeing, and/or experiencing. When we talk about hearing or reading, we are including second-hand evidence. By second-hand, we are referring to evidence that other people have spoken or written. That second-hand evidence is still valid evidence.

However, the amount of credibility we assign to the spoken or written evidence depends upon how much credibility we assign to the source of that evidence and how that evidence is transmitted to us.

Some atheists may object, saying they do not believe anything they cannot see or experience. Therefore, what other people teach cannot be trusted. In reality, that is foolishness. The vast majority of information anyone has accepted as fact—including what atheistic scientists have accepted as fact—has not come through seeing or experiencing. It has come through second-hand information, along with logical deductions and inferences made from second-hand information.

For example, the average citizen in the USA where I live has accepted as fact that there is a country in Africa called Egypt. Yet, most USA citizens have never seen Egypt with their own eyes or personally experienced it. They believe because it was taught to them, or they read about it, and/or have seen pictures. They believe Egypt exists because they have deemed as credible second-hand evidence.

What Is Faith?

So also most people have never seen with their own eyes whether or not:

- the people of Egypt have legs, arms, ears, etc.
- the people of Egypt eat, talk, reproduce, etc.
- there are in Egypt businesses, government, military, etc.
- there are in Egypt trees, crocodiles, birds, etc.
- the sky in Egypt is blue.

This list could go on indefinitely. A similar list could be developed for any country in the world.

We could make many more lists of things people believe though they have never seen or experienced them personally. For example, most people have never seen a person:

- do open-heart surgery,
- build a kitchen cabinet,
- make a watch,
- milk a goat,
- eat a monkey,
- kill an elephant,
- swim with sharks,
- eat a frog,
- assemble a computer, . . .

—but they believe these activities have taken place. And that is okay. It is rational to accept as true what people have been taught if they perceive the source of the information is credible.

This includes *all facts of history*. No one can go back in time and see or experience events that took place in the past.

They cannot go back one year or one thousand years to test or confirm what people did. They may be able to read about the past or examine artifacts left by people who lived in the past, but no one can actually use the scientific method on past events—whether those events took place 20 billion years ago or yesterday. At best, the only thing people can truly know about past events is what *possibly* happened.

Consider one more list of things people believe in without having seen, experienced, or tested with the scientific method. Most people believe but have never seen first-hand:

- an atom,
- cancer,
- their own immune system, or brain, or stomach,
- a virus,
- a dark hole,
- another galaxy,
- dust on the moon, . . .

Most scientists would argue that anyone who does not accept these as factual is foolish. Scientists expect everyone to believe what science has taught us.

Did you catch that? What science has "taught" us. Probably no one reading these words has conducted scientific experiments that prove there is dust on the moon, but all of us believe there is dust on the moon. Why do we believe? Because we have been taught. We heard, read, and saw photos. We accepted second-hand information.

Some atheists claim they cannot accept anything that cannot be tested via the scientific method. That is foolishness. Those same atheists will go eat at a restaurant, believing that the food will not be poisonous, without ever experimenting, observing, forming hypotheses, and testing the food. They put faith (trust) in the restaurant owner, the manager, the cooks, the servers, etc. They trust many people with their life, without using the scientific method.

I am not saying that is bad. It is just reality. It is the way people accumulate knowledge. The vast majority of what anyone knows and believes has not been observed and tested by that person. The information and evidence needed to produce faith (trust) comes primarily through other people.

MOST OF WHAT WE KNOW AND BELIEVE
HAS COME THROUGH OTHER PEOPLE

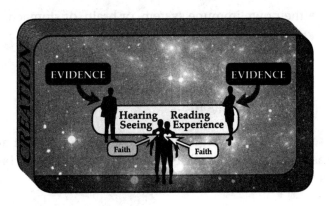

Point 4.13: Assigning Credibility to the Source

Everyone builds their life upon information they have learned through sources outside of themselves. It is rational to do so as long as the sources of information are deemed credible.

As children, we readily believe what our parents and teachers tell us. And that is okay. As explained in the previous point, most of what everyone believes was taught to them. It came to them through sources external to themselves, and they deemed the sources as credible. The older we get, however, the greater our inclination to evaluate the credibility of our sources.

Not only do we look at the credibility of the source but also to see if any new information fits into our developing worldview. To see this, it is helpful to think of a worldview as a big puzzle that each person puts together in their own mind throughout the course of their life. New information is like another puzzle piece. New information that does not fit into our worldview is like a puzzle piece that does not fit into the puzzle. If it does not fit, it seems irrational to us. If it does not fit, each of us tend to reject that new information as untrue.

Unfortunately, theists tend to reject the relevant sources and information that atheists accept. At the same time, atheists tend to reject the relevant sources and information the theists accept. This is a problem, and there are no easy answers. However, we can be aware of this.

We each employ our own worldview as the standard that we use to judge sources and new information. That judgment is an exercise of our intellect. Everyone uses their intellect as they consider if new information fits or does not fit into their worldview.

As one's worldview develops, they place **faith** in their worldview. Their heart (as the heart is defined in this book) comes at rest in one's conclusions about life. Those conclusions are the important concepts that are logically deduced from one's worldview.

It does not matter whether a person is an atheist, agnostic, or theist, every person has **faith** in their own worldview. Atheists

What Is Faith?

have faith in their worldview just as much as theists have **faith** in their worldview. They both have so much **faith**, they build their entire life upon the conclusions to which their worldview leads.

This is important. Atheists often accuse theists of building their life on faith, while implying that they themselves do not build on faith. In reality, everyone has **faith**. The question is simply what do people put their **faith** in?

This adds one more point to our growing understanding of faith.

UNDERSTANDING OF FAITH

Western Philosophical	Biblically-derived
1. A function of the intellect	1. A function of the heart
2. Mental assent to ideas	2. Trust
3. Irrational	3. Rational
4. Blind leap	4. Produced by:
	hearing,
	reading,
	seeing,
	experiencing
5. No evidence	5. Based on evidence
6. No association with heart	6. Change in heart
7. **Only theists have faith**	7. **All people have faith**

This discussion on faith, evidence, and credibility has been necessary so we can talk about the evidence for atheism / agnosticism versus theism. In Section 5, we will be examining the evidence / proof for atheism versus theism. We cannot communicate effectively about that without first clearly identifying what we mean by these key terms.

Point 4.14: Where Does the Bible Fit?

In Section 5, I will not use the Bible as evidence / proof for or against the existence of God, but here it is worth mentioning that book because over two billion Christians in the world do assign some credibility to the Bible and it does serve as one source of evidence for their **faith**.

The Bible was written by people. Over 40 authors over the course of over 1,500 years recorded what they understood as their experiences with God. Those people wrote down their testimonies of what they experienced and how they understood those experiences.

THE BIBLE IS WRITTEN TESTIMONIES OF WHAT OTHER PEOPLE UNDERSTOOD AS THEIR EXPERIENCES WITH GOD

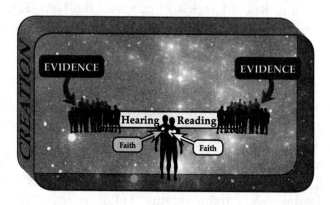

The Bible is second-hand evidence.[46] But as explained in point 4.12, almost everything we accept as evidence comes to us as second-hand evidence.

Atheists have worked hard to dissuade people from accepting as true what is written in the Bible, and I cannot

46 Many will refer to it as third, fourth, fifth, etc., -hand evidence.

prove the validity of the Bible in these short pages. However, I can offer some brief points explaining how the Bible is not as untrustworthy as atheists want us to believe.

Atheists ridicule the Bible by stating or implying it is full of errors. Students at universities are often given a list of proposed errors in the Bible. Rarely do the students have time to investigate those proposed errors for themselves. *Unfortunately, students do not spend equal amounts of time studying the opposing arguments.*

There are many books written by scholars who value the Bible, explaining how every one of those proposed errors is not really an error but a misunderstanding by people who do not understand the language and cultural settings in which the Bible writers lived. After reading several of those books and after learning Koine Greek so I can read the New Testament in the language in which it was originally written, I have more doubts about the atheists than I do about the Bible.

Even people who do not believe God was involved in the writing of the Bible ought to recognize some value in the book simply because of its human authorship. Among the authors are some of the most influential people in history, such as Abraham, Moses, Elijah, David, Solomon, Isaiah, Daniel, Matthew, Mark, Luke, John, Peter, and Paul. None of these leaders were light-weights. Followers of Christianity, Judaism, and Islam all consider Abraham their forefather, which means over half of the world's population today looks to him. Furthermore, the words and thoughts of Jesus are recorded in the Bible.

The collection of writings that we know as the Bible is invaluable simply because of the historical figures who contributed to those writings. If we had a similar collection of the writings of other great historical leaders, each explaining their understanding of God and how he influenced them, that collection would be priceless. Even if there were some errors discovered in that book, it would still be studied and valued by scholars around the world.

The Bible is such a collection. Yet, all of the authors of the Bible wrote about the same God. They recorded what they believed God communicated with them. They wrote of their experiences with God and testified to miracles that they accredited to the One God.

Of course, atheists cannot believe any of the miracles recorded in the Bible, because their worldview will not permit it. For the rest of us, it is not irrational to believe in miracles. All that is necessary for miracles is the existence of God.

Point 4.15: Is the Resurrection of Jesus Evidence / Proof?

What does the Bible tells us about Jesus? Consider looking at Jesus from the perspective that Jesus is presented in the Bible as, at least, a representative sent from God. If Jesus really did work miracles, that adds credibility to what He taught.

Sometimes critics make unfounded statements such as, "The Bible is the only writing of the period that talks about Jesus." In reality, there are several writings outside of the Bible from the first and second centuries that talk about Jesus. I could take time to discuss those writings, but they are readily available to anyone willing to do a quick search on the internet.[47]

---

47 Among those websites are these: https://coldcasechristianity.com/writings/is-there-any-evidence-for-jesus-outside-the-bible/ Retrieved April 2019. https://www.bethinking.org/jesus/ancient-evidence-for-jesus-from-non-christian-sources Retrieved April 2019. https://www.josh.org/evidence-jesus-lived/ Retrieved April 2019.

What Is Faith?

Plus, the Bible itself is not one book, but a whole library of books. For example, there are four different accounts of the life of Jesus, written by Matthew, Mark, Luke, and John. They each wrote their own account, so rather than thinking the Bible is the only book talking about Jesus, it is more accurate to say there are four different historic books that each gives an account of the life, death, and resurrection of Jesus. Long after those four books were written, they were compiled and included in the Bible.

In addition, there are 23 other historical writings in the New Testament from the first century. All 23 of those writings explain the implications of Jesus' life upon the early believers. In other words, the New Testament is a library of 27 books. So the Bible is not one book. The New Testament is a collection of 27 books written in the first century all talking about Jesus.[48]

If you had 27 books on your library shelf, all from the first century and all talking about one famous individual, wouldn't you give those books some credibility?

Most of the writers of the New Testament claimed to be eye-witnesses of the resurrection of Jesus, and we should assign more credibility to them than the average Joe walking the street. More credibility because of what they risked for their testimonies. Jesus had twelve men who walked with him during his three-plus years of ministry. Apart from Judas who betrayed Jesus then committed suicide, we have historical records explaining how the remaining eleven men were all tortured for their testimony about Jesus, and none of them recanted from their testimony that they saw Jesus after

---

48 For many years, liberal scholars argued that few, if any, of the New Testament writings were actually written before 100 AD. Today, that is a difficult view to continue holding because in recent years many writings of the Church fathers who lived in the first and second centuries have been discovered. Those writings, most of which are available to anyone willing to investigate, contain more than 80,000 quotations from the New Testament, proving those New Testament books were written much earlier than previously thought.

his death and resurrection. In my thinking, unwavering testimonies while undergoing torture adds some credibility to their statements.

Point 4.16: Proof Provided by the Prophets

In the Bible, we also have writings produced by individuals called prophets who lived hundreds of years before Jesus and who accurately foretold details about Jesus, including when and where he would be born, how he would die, and how he would resurrect after being dead for three days:

When he would be born—Daniel 9:24-25

Where he would be born—Micah 5:2

When he would die—Daniel 9:26

How he would die by crucifixion—Psalm 22:16-18

How he would resurrect from the dead—Psalm 16:10, 30:3

Those prophecies so accurately predict details about Jesus, that for over one hundred years atheistic scholars claimed the prophecies had to have been written after Jesus lived. Indeed, atheists have no alternative explanation but that explanation was proven false when thousands of ancient scrolls, now known as the *Dead Sea Scrolls*, were discovered between 1947-1956. Among those scrolls are copies of the Old Testament (Hebrew Scriptures),[49] including the books of the prophets detailing the future life of Jesus. Today, many of those manuscripts, dating over 100 years before Jesus was born, are being displayed in various museums and public locations around the world. I have seen them with my own eyes. To anyone willing to examine them, they are evidence that something greater than human wisdom was at work foretelling of events to come in the future.

---

49 All of the writings of the Old Testament (Hebrew Scriptures) were discovered except one small writing called the *Book of Esther*.

What Is Faith?

Point 4.17: Faith Changes Life and Behavior

Now let's turn our eyes back upon **faith** and consider the *value of faith*. Does **faith** make any difference in the life of a person?

From the historic philosophical perspective, faith in God has little to no value. This corresponds to the philosophical view that sees faith as a function of the intellect. It is a mental assent to the existence of an unknowable God, who belongs in a far away, unreachable world. In accordance with that view, faith in God is not a big deal. Faith does not really change a person or make a person's life better. Therefore, for atheists / agnostics, there is no reason to give much energy or thought to the subject of faith.

Some atheists / agnostics will assign a small, insignificant value to the theist's faith, saying faith may offer a framework for theists to organize their thoughts. As such, the theist's faith may help them make sense of the world and cope with the problems they face.

However, atheists / agnostics do not see that such faith would make any significant changes in the behavior or life of a person. So it is a non-issue for most of them.

In contrast, the biblically-derived understanding of **faith** sees **faith** as changing *everything* about a person's life. This is true because **faith** is a function of the heart, and as explained, from the heart "flow all the springs of life" (Proverbs 4:23). With the heart as the control center of human nature, a change in the heart results in a change in nature and behavior.

The concept that **faith** results in corresponding behavior is a consistent theme of the Bible. The Bible writer, James, explained how faith that does not produce good works is not true **faith**.[50] Whatever happens in the heart changes the whole person.

The association of **faith** and behavior is further strengthened within the biblically-derived cosmology. A God who is close, filling the natural world, is seen as much more involved with and influential in the lives of individuals than a god who is unknowable and unreachable.

I once tried to explain this concept to an atheist but he had no frame of reference for the concept that **faith** determines behavior. I tried to emphasize my point by explaining how we should be able to identify a theist by examining their bank statements. Of course, this is not true for someone who simply gives mental assent to a distant god's existence, but theists who have true **faith** will orient their life toward pleasing God who is very close. That orientation results in radical changes in the lifestyle and priorities of an individual, including how they spend their money.

The atheist to whom I tried to explain this had no frame of reference for **faith** that changes behavior. According to his understanding, the best faith in God can offer is a reference point to an unknowable, distant god, who really does not exist. Such a reference point may help the theist cope with the problems of life, but according to the atheist, any belief in God is belief in a myth which leads to misunderstandings and confusion.

This identifies another major distinction between the philosophical understanding of faith and the biblically-derived understanding of **faith**.

---

50 James 2:14-26.

What Is Faith?

Western Philosophical	Biblically-derived
1. A function of the intellect	1. A function of the heart
2. Mental assent to ideas	2. Trust
3. Irrational	3. Rational
4. Blind leap	4. Produced by: hearing, reading, seeing, experiencing
5. No evidence	5. Based on evidence
6. No association with heart	6. Change in heart
7. Only theists have faith	7. All people have faith
8. A reference point for (mis)understanding	8. Changes behavior
9. Little to no value	9. Very valuable

Point 4.18: Faith Creates a Trust/Bond

Finally, the biblically-derived understanding sees that **faith** creates a bond between the trusting person and the person in whom trust is placed.[51] **Faith** creates a connection. Furthermore, the bond allows strength and life to flow between the two individuals.

For example, students must have **faith** (trust) in their teachers in order to receive the greatest benefit from their teachers. Athletes need to put **faith** (trust) in their coach in order to be fully strengthened by their coach's instructions and encouragement. If, indeed, the student and athlete place **faith** in their leader, they will benefit from the bond and the flow of life and strength.

For this reason, when a trusted leader fails, as in the sense of

---

51 Rather than just with a person, a bond may also be created by faith in an institution, a scientific principle, a machine, etc.

no longer being trustworthy, it can feel like the trusting individual got kicked in the stomach. There is a breaking of a bond and strength ceases to flow to the trusting individual. On the other hand, if trusted individuals remain solid and trustworthy, they remain an anchor and source of life for the trusting person.

FAITH CREATES A BOND WITH THE PERSON IN WHOM ONE TRUSTS

This same dynamic happens between God and a person who has faith in God.

BIBLICALLY-DERIVED UNDERSTANDING:
FAITH AND LOVE CREATE A BOND WITH GOD

What Is Faith?

So this adds two more points to our biblically-derived understanding of **faith**.

Western Philosophical	Biblically-derived
1. A function of the intellect	1. A function of the heart
2. Mental assent to ideas	2. Trust
3. Irrational	3. Rational
4. Blind leap	4. Produced by: hearing, reading, seeing, experiencing
5. No evidence	5. Based on evidence
6. No association with heart	6. Change in heart
7. Only theists have faith	7. All people have faith
8. A reference point for (mis)understanding	8. Changes behavior
9. Little to no value	9. Very valuable
10. Creates nothing	10. Creates a bond
	11. Allows Strength and Life to Flow

From the biblical perspective, **faith** and **love** are similar in many ways. Both are functions of the heart. Both create a bond.

Faith and **love** also allow strength and life to flow. This is the biblically-derived understanding of **faith** and **love**.

Summary of Section Four

The biblically-derived understanding of **faith** is very different than the philosophically-derived understanding of faith.

For true **faith**, evaluation of the evidence must be followed by a corresponding change of heart. **Faith** in God is trust in God, creating a bond that allows strength and life to flow

Where Does the Evidence Lead?
Atheism or Theism?

Faith is built on evidence/proof. Now it is time we see if there is enough evidence/proof to justify putting **faith** in God.

Point 5.1: Atheism Is Always an Assumption

We have identified at least six assumptions along the philo-sophical path leading to atheism/agnosticism.

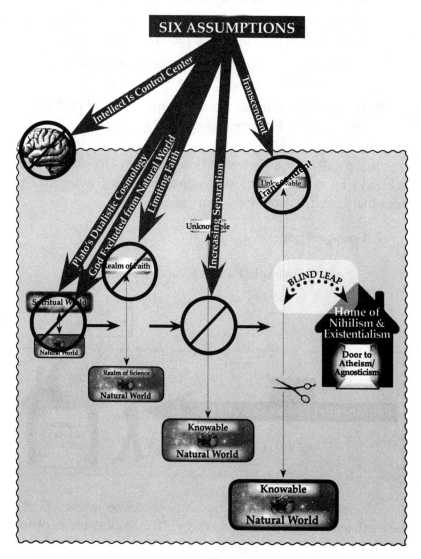

Where Does the Evidence Lead? Atheism or Theism?

All six of these assumptions are necessary building blocks for the philosophical progression:

1. The intellect is the control center of human nature
2. Plato's dualistic cosmology
3. Plato's exclusion of God from the natural world
4. Associating faith with the spiritual world & defining it as mental ascent to certain ideas for which there is no evidence
5. The increasing separation of the spiritual world from the natural world
6. Declaring the spiritual world as transcendent, then defining transcendent as unknowable and unprovable

To top it all off, the Western philosophical progression requires a blind leap to take the most significant step into atheism. The idea that God does not exist is pure assumption.

7. God does not exist

ATHEISM IS BASED ON NO EVIDENCE

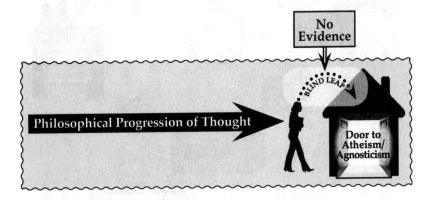

Atheists admit that it is impossible to prove God's non-existence. They word it this way: "It is impossible to prove a negative." This is true, but they usually make that statement as if it gets them off of the hook. In other words, they say, "It is impossible to prove a negative," suggesting we should just accept atheism as fact and move on to discuss other subjects.

Wait a minute! Let's not go so fast. Think about what they are saying. They have no evidence, yet they believe there is no God. That violates any logical search for truth in both philosophical and scientific pursuits. Atheism is not the default setting. Both philosophy and science claim to only accept as true that which can be proven. God's non-existence cannot be proven.

For this reason, atheism always requires a blind leap. It is a logically indefensible view.

A logical person must seriously question the validity of an entire progression of thought if it is built on even one assumption. I do not want to sound sarcastic but, to truth-seekers, seven assumptions qualify a progression of thought as laughable.

Even more assumptions in the philosophical progression will be noted in this section.

Point 5.2: Is This Evidence for Theism?

Now consider if there is any evidence to support theism.

When I refer to *"evidence,"* I will be distinguishing it from *"proof." Evidence* points to a certain conclusion, but evidence does not eliminate all doubt about that conclusion. Several pieces of evidence all pointing to the same conclusion result in more confidence in that conclusion but that still does not qualify as proof.

Where Does the Evidence Lead? Atheism or Theism?

Proof is a stronger claim than evidence. Proof requires unquestionable steps of logic such as a mathematical statement, similar to, 2 + 2 = 4. When known facts *prove* some conclusion, there will be no doubts about that conclusion. Nor will there be any possible alternative explanations.

With this distinction between evidence and proof in mind, consider a survey done by Frank Sulloway and Michael Shermer in 1998. They asked 10,000 Americans, "Why do you believe in God?" The most common answers had to do with "good design," "natural beauty," "perfection," "complexity of the universe," and "experience of God in everyday life."[52] Each of these five answers is based on reason and evidence:

1. Good design
2. Natural beauty
3. Perfection
4. Complexity of the universe
5. Experience of God in everyday life

There is a spectrum concerning how much credibility people assign to each of these as evidence / proof. At one end of the spectrum are all atheists and some theists who reject any of these as evidence. At the other end of the spectrum are some theists who take one or more of these as proof of God's existence.

Different People's Evaluation of Evidence Falls Across a Spectrum

| No Evidence of God's Existence | ← | Proof of God's Existence |

52 Cited in David Marshall, *The Truth Behind the New Atheism* (Eugene, OR: Harvest House Publishers, 2007), pp. 23-24.

The important question is this: "How do *you* value these five things theists point to as evidence?" This is not a case of $2 + 2 = 4$. Instead, it is similar to a case in a court of law and every person in the jury has to decide to what verdict the evidence points.

Point 5.3: Atheists Base Their Rejection on Assumption

For years, atheists have been rejecting, even ridiculing, theists who claim to have evidence or proof for God's existence. Think about that for a minute. On what basis do atheist's reject the claims of theists?

Consider the fifth reason given above for why theists say they believe in God: "experience of God in everyday life."

"Experiences" can refer to a great variety of things, from the individual's mystical sense of God's presence to the more substantial experience like what Paul was reported in the Bible to have experienced: struck by a blinding light, knocked off of his donkey, and talked to by an audible voice from heaven.[53]

Atheists have to reject all reports of such experiences or at least reject that such experiences are related to God. Why do atheists reject them? Well, their rejection cannot be based on evidence because it is impossible for any atheist to know whether or not all of those testimonies are true or false.

An atheist may personally have a theist friend who testifies to have encountered God and that atheist may reject his friend's testimony. That is reasonable because the atheist knows his friend and, therefore, may know if his friend is a reliable witness. To reject someone's testimony because they are unreliable is a rational thing to do.

---

53 Acts 9:1-6.

However, there are millions and millions of Christians in the world who claim to have experienced God. Atheists have to reject *all of their testimonies* about experiencing God.

The reason atheists reject the testimonies of those millions and millions of theists is not because they have personally gotten to know all of those millions of theists then decided those people are unreliable witnesses. That would be impossible.

The real reason atheists reject the testimony of those millions and millions of theists is because of their own assumption that God does not exist. Think about that. Atheists have no evidence that God does not exist. There are millions of people testifying that they have experienced God, but atheists must reject what all those millions of people are saying, not because they have evidence for the opposing view, but because they have an assumption that God does not exist. Their assumption is what makes them reject the testimony of millions of people. That is logically indefensible.

I am *not* saying we should uncritically accept the testimony of everyone who claims to have experienced God. What I am saying is there are millions and millions of theists who claim to have experienced God and *the assumption that there is no God is not a rational reason to reject all of their testimonies*.

Point 5.4: I Count Zero to Five

Because people have to decide for themselves, I have to decide for myself. For me, other people's testimonies are not proof of God's existence. However, those testimonies do carry *some* credibility.

Of course, there is a certain percentage of impressionable, crazy people who are not very credible. But there is also a certain percentage that are intelligent and level-headed. I have listened to a lot of their testimonies about personal experiences they say they have had with God. Some of them seem significant. I can't discard them all as the product of overactive imaginations or insanity.

Personally, I give *some* credibility to each of the five things theists point to as evidence for God's existence:

1. Good design
2. Natural beauty
3. Perfection
4. Complexity of the universe
5. Experience of God in everyday life

When I weigh the evidence, I do see *some* weight in all five points. Together they add up to more evidence. At the same time, I know atheists have no evidence for the non-existence of God. That means, so far, I count atheists zero and theists five.

WEIGH THE EVIDENCE

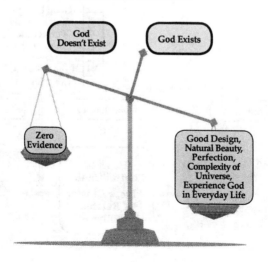

Where Does the Evidence Lead? Atheism or Theism?

What do you think? You are certainly free to disagree with me. You can also consider the viewpoints of others, but their judgment will only outweigh your own judgment if you place more value on their judgment than you do in your own. You don't need to do that. In fact, *it is illogical for you to place more value in someone else's judgment unless you believe they have more credibility than you do yourself.*

Point 5.5: Theism Is Not a Blind Leap

As we stated, some people do not give any credibility to any of the five areas that theists point to as evidence for God's existence. That does not change the fact that millions of theists can and do offer them as evidence. Because millions of theists see these as evidence of God, those theists are not taking a blind leap. Those theists are basing their decision to believe in God on what they consider evidence.

THEISM IS BASED ON EVIDENCE

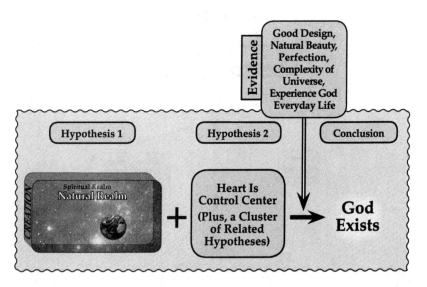

Modern atheists accuse theists of believing without evidence, but when atheists do that, they are misrepresenting the view of theists. Anyone is free to accept or reject the evidence, but the idea that theists believe without evidence is pure fiction.

It is the atheists who believe without any evidence.

Of course, some atheists may object to this, saying, "We are atheists because God has not proven his existence." But the absence of proof for God is not proof of God's non-existence.

Other atheists may object saying, "I cannot believe in God because there is so much evil in the world." But that is not evidence of God's non-existence. It is merely evidence that God does not act the way they expect him to act. That is an entirely different discussion—worth having at another time, but it has *nothing* to do with God's existence or non-existence.

Some atheists will also ask questions such as, "Why are people who claim to believe in God so bad?" As explained earlier (point 3.27), such questions are "detour questions," causing the listener to chase a bone in a direction away from the real question, "Does God exist?" Anyone who actually faces the real question will conclude there is no evidence for the non-existence of God but theists do offer evidence for their belief in God. Therefore, atheism requires blind faith. Theism does not.

Point 5.6: Existence of the World as Evidence of a Creator

There is more evidence upon which theists base their **faith**. In fact, we could make the list much longer, but I am hesitant to talk about those additions because doing so may actually make the theist's position weaker in the mind of the reader. This is true because atheists may attack the weakest point in the list, and readers may project that weakness upon the entire list. Hence, remaining with strong points often states the position more clearly.

However, we have not yet dealt with one of the most obvious areas of evidence. We need to talk about *the existence of the world as evidence of a creator*.

Whenever theists mention this, atheists are usually quick to object, saying, "It is just as rational to think the world has always existed as it is to think a creator created it." Indeed, that is the only logical alternative explanation for why the world exists. Either a creator created the world or the world has always existed.[54]

Atheists often offer their answer—the world always existed—thinking or implying they have destroyed the view of theists. But they have not. An alternative view does not destroy or negate another view. Both views still stand as possibilities.

Only Two Options

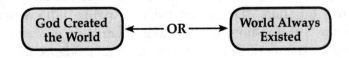

So which of the two views is correct?

There is *no* scientific evidence that the world has always existed—zero evidence. In contrast, there is evidence that the world was created. Recall the five things theists commonly give as evidence of God's existence. Of those five, the first four also

---

54 Some have proposed a third alternative—that the world created itself, but that is not a true alternative, because the world could not create itself unless there already existed laws by which it could create itself. In that case, the laws would have had to be created by a creator or the laws would have had to always exist. That puts us right back to only the two options.

apply as evidence for believing God created the world.

$$\text{Evidence that God created the world} \begin{cases} \text{1. Good design} \\ \text{2. Natural beauty} \\ \text{3. Perfection} \\ \text{4. Complexity of the universe} \end{cases}$$

5. Experience of God in everyday life

In addition to the evidence given above, there is scientific evidence that the world came into existence at a point in time. Most scientists who believe the big bang theory have accepted that the universe began approximately 13.7 billion years ago. They came up with this number by observing how the universe is expanding, then extrapolating back in time to estimate when the expanding universe would have existed as one point.

If the world came into existence at a point in time, there must have been a creator. This is exactly what many scientists have concluded. One college physics professor came to ask me about God after he embraced the big bang theory. He said, "You guys (meaning you people who talk about God) must be very busy now (meaning now that the big bang theory has become popular)." Indeed, many scientists, who were previously atheists, changed their view to theism as a result of concluding that the world came into existence at a point in time.

You do not have to accept the world as evidence / proof of God's existence, but it is worth noting that many scientists now do. For me, the existence of the world has always been proof of the creator's existence. I will explain, but first, we must expose another assumption (number 8) in the Western philosophical progression of thought.

Point 5.7: The Assumption that God Is Hiding

At the foundation of Western philosophy is another assumption: if God exists, *he cannot or will not reveal himself in any irrefutable manner.* This assumption is so pervasive it has spread beyond the secular philosophical world and been embraced by many modern Christians.

When Western philosophy labeled the spiritual world and God as "transcendent," leaders included in that label the idea that God, if he exists, will never irrefutably prove his existence to people who exist in the natural world.

PHILOSOPHICAL ASSUMPTION:
GOD, IF HE EXISTS,
WILL NOT IRREFUTABLY REVEAL HIMSELF TO PEOPLE

This concept was developed in the context of discussing the nature of God. God was portrayed as not wanting to reveal himself in an irrefutable manner lest people be coerced into believing in him. Instead, God, if he exists, was seen as distant and concealed, choosing out of his infinite wisdom to only suggest his existence so people would have the freedom to willingly respond to his love.

That understanding of God's distance and concealment was closely tied to the philosophical understanding that faith always requires a blind leap. Both of these concepts are contrary to the biblically-derived understanding of God and faith.

Point 5.8: The God of the Bible Does Prove His Existence

The concept that God is distant and concealing himself is contrary to the concept of the Christian God revealed in the Bible. As I explain this, I am not implying that you have to believe in the Christian God. I am just identifying who the Christian God is, and in doing so, showing you how the Christian God is different than the philosophically-derived god.

The God revealed in the Bible does not exist in a faraway transcendent world. He exists in a spiritual realm that fills the heavens and earth. *He is here, all around us.*

Furthermore, *the God of the Bible wants to reveal himself and he does reveal himself—sometimes irrefutably!*

To see this, first consider the revelation of God as described in the Old Testament. The Bible tells about how God proved that he was with Moses by working miracles before Pharaoh and all of the Egyptians.[55] They saw those miracles as *proof.*

---

55 Exodus 7-13.

Where Does the Evidence Lead? Atheism or Theism?

Next consider when God descended upon Mount Sinai and revealed himself to the over two million Hebrews gathered at the bottom of the mountain.[56] They had *proof.*

In several Bible passages, angels are reported to have appeared to people. Other times certain people were taken into the throne room of God or heard his audible voice. From such reports, we can conclude that the people who wrote the Bible believed God at times provided irrefutable evidence his existence.

In the New Testament, we read about the most obvious proof of God's existence, in that God came into the physical world in human flesh in Jesus. Jesus came to reveal who God is.

THE GOD REVEALED IN THE BIBLE
CAME INTO THE NATURAL WORLD

The God of the Bible worked miracles through Jesus. The blind received sight, the lame walked, the deaf heard, and the dying were raised from their deathbeds. The people reported to have experienced these miracles accepted them as proof that God was working through Jesus.

---

56 Exodus 19:16-20:21.

Consider again the biblical report of Paul being struck by a blinding light, knocked off of his donkey and spoken to from heaven. Paul had *proof*.

Then recall the most noted miracle reported in the Bible which is the resurrection of Jesus from the dead. When Paul was speaking to the philosophers in the city of Athens, he said:

> God . . . has fixed a day in which He will judge the world . . . having furnished proof to all men by raising Him from the dead.
>
> [emphasis mine] Acts 17:30-31

When Paul was debating with the philosophers of Athens, he argued that the resurrection of Jesus was *proof*.

You may not accept the resurrection as true, but what we are determining here is what the Bible writers thought. The Bible writers saw that God provided proof of His existence.

Point 5.9: Proof Does Not Coerce People to Believe

So why do some people say God would never reveal himself irrefutably? Well, it could be because they don't believe the Bible. It could also be because they do not see God revealing himself today as he was reported to do in the Bible times.

Another possibility is that they have a misunderstanding of the nature of God. They wrongly think God would never reveal himself irrefutably because he does not want to force anyone to believe in him. Instead, they believe God wants people to have freewill in their decision to believe.

That is a misunderstanding of the nature of God, and it is closely tied to a misunderstanding of faith. Let me explain.

Where Does the Evidence Lead? Atheism or Theism?

As I have been saying, faith is not a function of the intellect. It is a function of the heart. For this reason, people may have absolute, irrefutable proof of God's existence in their intellect and still not have **faith** in their heart. God does not coerce people to believe in him, but he can and does at times coerce people to know he exists. The place free will comes into play in the development of **faith** is at the level of the heart.

BIBLICALLY-DERIVED UNDERSTANDING:
GOD MAY PROVE HIS EXISTENCE TO THE INTELLECT,
BUT FAITH IS A FUNCTION OF THE HEART

Point 5.10: The Historic Philosophical Change In Proof

The reason we just discussed the possibility of God providing irrefutable evidence (proof) of his existence is because we need that understanding to talk about creation as evidence / proof of God's existence.

Before the Enlightenment (the 1700s), most Western philosophers accepted the existence of the world as evidence / proof of God's existence. After the Enlightenment (after 1850), most philosophers rejected the world as evidence / proof of a creator.

What changed?

The evidence/proof did not change, but the interpretation of the evidence/proof changed. And how were things reinterpreted? Most significantly, the spiritual world was separated from the natural world and the spiritual world was labeled "transcendent."

Once someone embraces the assumption that god is transcendent, in the sense of being unable or unwilling to cross a spiritual/natural separation, they must reject any irrefutable evidence that god exists. Their assumption that god is transcendent makes them reject any evidence/proof of god's existence.

In reality, the God who is revealed in the Bible is not transcendent in the way Western philosophy describes. The God of the Bible is not separated, unreachable, and unknowable. The God of the Bible is very different than the philosophically-derived god.

The philosophically-derived concept could be accurately called the "philosophically-engineered concept of god." It is designed and engineered to be unprovable. This is true because labeling god "transcendent" creates a cyclic argument. An unprovable (transcendent) God is unprovable. By definition of that god, there can be no proof of his existence.

It would do no good for me to try to give you evidence or proof for the existence of the philosophically-engineered god, because that is impossible, and besides, I don't believe in that god. The only God for which I can offer you evidence/proof is the Christian God who is shown in the Bible as existing in our midst and, at times, reveals himself irrefutably.

Where Does the Evidence Lead? Atheism or Theism?

Point 5.11: God Provided Proof/Evidence of His Existence

The God who is revealed in the Bible can and does provide evidence/proof of his existence. Not only were the miracles recorded in the Bible understood as evidence/proof of God's existence, but Paul also understood that the existence of the world is proof of God's existence.

Earlier, we mentioned Paul's teaching in Romans 1:20, about the world revealing the existence and nature of God:

> *For since the creation of the world His invisible attributes, His eternal power and divine nature, have been clearly seen, being understood through what has been made so that they are without excuse.*
>
> Romans 1:20

Before the Enlightenment, most philosophers and theologians understood Paul's statement here to mean *the existence of the world is proof of God's existence*. After the Enlightenment, most philosophers and theologians reinterpreted Paul's words. They either rejected Paul's explanation as wrong or said, "Paul did not really mean the world is proof of God's existence."

And what was Paul actually saying in Romans 1? In that passage, Paul explained that the world is such convincing proof of God's existence, that every human being is "without excuse." In the context, Paul said God's existence is so obvious, so "clearly seen," no one has an excuse for disbelieving or living as if God does not exist. Paul was 100 percent convinced that the world's existence is proof of God's existence.

This was not only Paul's understanding of the world, but the Psalmist also declared:

The heavens are telling of the glory of God;
And their expanse is declaring the work of His hands.

Psalm 9:1

Notice that I am not using this Bible verse or Paul's words in Romans 1 to prove God exists. Rather, I am showing you how the Bible writers thought. They thought the existence of the world is proof of a creator.

It is not an illogical way of thinking . . .

- A watch is proof that a watchmaker existed.
- A book is proof that an author existed.
- A house is proof that a carpenter existed.
- A car is proof that a car maker existed.
- Creation is proof that a creator existed.

The Bible writers not only saw the world as proof of a creator but what God created reveals "His invisible attributes, His eternal power and divine nature." According to the Bible writer, the world reveals that the creator is powerful, imaginative, and glorious.

Point 5.12: I See the Existence of the World as Proof

I agree with Paul and the Psalmist that the world is proof of God's existence.

Of course, most philosophically-trained people will disagree with me, but so what? Just because some philosophers have rejected the world as evidence / proof of a creator does not mean I have to reject it. In fact, it is illogical for me to reject something just because others have rejected it unless I put more faith in their judgment than in my own judgment.

Where Does the Evidence Lead? Atheism or Theism?

The truth is I am skeptical of the atheistic philosophers who have controlled Western philosophical thought since the Enlightenment. The reasons I am skeptical were pointed out in Section 1 and 3: they built upon Plato's assumed cosmology, excluded God from the natural world, created a greater and greater distance between the spiritual and natural worlds, and labeled the spiritual world as transcendent. How can I place credibility in their conclusion when I am convinced all of these assumptions are false? Furthermore, I am convinced their progression of thought is distorted by the motives of their heart (explained in points 3.32-3.36). I can't trust their judgment.

Another reason I cannot trust the judgment of the atheistic philosophers is because their progression of thought is designed to blind their eyes to the evidence / proof. That statement calls for an explanation.

Philosophers are known for their ability to use their skills at logical argument to the end that they can deny the existence of anything. For example, philosophers can go through a series of mental gymnastics to build a progression of thought that will lead them to deny your existence even if you are standing directly in front of them. Such a progression of thought may go as follows:

1. I can see that you are standing in front of me.

2. However, I may be sleeping and dreaming that you are standing in front of me. Or I may be experiencing a hallucination.

3. So, I don't know if you are really standing in front of me.

This progression of thought does not determine whether or not you are actually there. The progression simply makes the philosopher unable to know if you are there. The progression blinds the philosopher from accepting physical reality as true.

Such a progression is similar to the one I told you about earlier (point 3.24), which formed as I worked on my Bachelor of Science degree. I could not see the beauty in nature because my studies had formed a progression of thought that caused me to analyze nature scientifically rather than aesthetically. Furthermore, definitions of key words changed my perception such as when I labeled a blue spruce tree, *Picea pungens glauca*. The progression of thought and the words that I learned at the university did not change the beauty of nature. They merely hindered me from seeing the beauty.

Every progression of thought changes a person's focus. It allows them to see certain things and hinders them from seeing other things.

Point 5.13: It's a Mystery

Consider the historical philosophical progression.

1. Starting with Plato's cosmology, making it impossible to envision God within the natural world.
2. Creating a greater and greater separation, making it harder to envision God close to the natural world.
3. Defining faith as mental assent to ideas for which there is no evidence, and hence, excluding the possibility of finding evidence for faith.
4. Labeling the spiritual world as transcendent, then defining transcendent as unknowable and unprovable, making the god who may exist in that transcendent world unprovable.

Finally, the philosophers pulled the blinds closed on God by declaring God is a mystery. They used the word "transcendent" rather than mystery, but it served the same purpose as the word "mystery" does. Let me explain.

Where Does the Evidence Lead? Atheism or Theism?

Consider the blinding influence that results from declaring something is a "mystery." Of course, there may be some true mysteries about certain subjects. However, labeling something a mystery typically serves to end all further investigation and discussion about that subject.

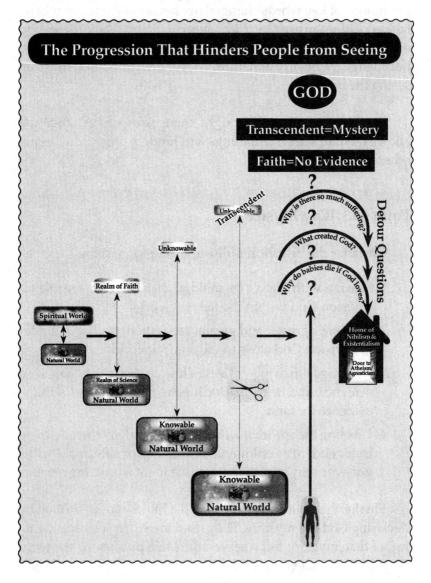

True science will never label something a "mystery." Scientists may say a certain question cannot be answered at the present time, but true science never slams the door closed on further investigation.

Once a respected teacher declares something is a mystery, those who follow her teaching tend to stop thinking about that subject. Since the teacher said it is a mystery, there is no use to continue trying to figure it out.

The historic philosophical progression labeled the spiritual world transcendent. Then leaders reinforced the mystery by saying faith has no evidence.

Why did we take the time to explain this? Because it reveals how Western philosophy blinds the eyes of individuals. Their progression of thought is designed to blind their eyes to any evidence / proof of God's existence.

Point 5.14: What Is Going On in the University?

So, why is it that a young woman can enter a university believing in God and four years later come out not knowing if God exists?

There are two possibilities.

Number one, it is possible that before that young woman went to the university she was just deceived about God's existence, but during the university training the deception cleared up and she realized there is no evidence for God's existence.

Number two, the young woman went into the university

191

knowing God exists, but during her university training, she received a progression of thought that blinded her from seeing the evidence / proof of God's existence.

Either of these scenarios is logically possible. I have concluded the second scenario is what is happening: people go into a university believing in God but come out not believing in God because they have been given a progression of thought that blinds them from seeing the evidence / proof of God's existence.

Point 5.15: A Progression of Thought Can Enable Sight

As already stated, every progression of thought changes a person's focus. It *blinds* a person from seeing some things and *opens their eyes to see* other things. Now let's talk about a person's eyes being opened to see.

While I was earning my BS degree in Wildlife Management, I learned how to accurately identify different animal tracks. For example, I could easily distinguish the tracks left by a bobcat from the tracks of any other animal. Therefore, when I came across a set of bobcat tracks in the wild, I had evidence that a bobcat had been at that location.

I not only had evidence of a bobcat's existence but in some cases I had proof. Clear bobcat tracks are so distinctive to the trained eye that there is no possible alternative explanation. Therefore, if the tracks were clearly imprinted in the mud or snow, plus there were no human tracks nearby showing that it was impossible that a human formed those bobcat tracks so as to deceive me, then I would know without any doubt that those tracks were made by a bobcat. In those cases, I had proof that a bobcat had been there.

Another person, who did not learn how to identify animal tracks, could see the same bobcat tracks I saw but they would not have evidence or proof that a bobcat had been present. If they had a little bit of training in identifying animal tracks, they may have evidence but not irrefutable evidence. On the other hand, if they had the same training I had, the tracks may qualify as not only evidence but also proof that the bobcat that been there.

The point is this: some progressions of thought can enable a person to see evidence or proof that other people cannot see.

Point 5.16: The Philosophers Can't See

As I explained, I can look at tracks left in nature and tell you if they were made by a bobcat or not. Someone without the thought progression I have could look at the same tracks and not know if they were made by a bobcat.

Now think how foolish it would be for the person without my training to accuse me not being able to identify bobcat tracks. They don't have a progression of thought that reveals whether or not tracks are made by a bobcat, but they have the audacity to tell me that I can't identify those tracks either.

Their inability to see the evidence does not give them the right to tell me that I can't see the evidence. In fact, they have no logical way of knowing whether or not I can actually see the evidence / proof.

In the same way, no philosopher can logically say whether any other person can see evidence / proof of God's existence. They may be able to logically say of themselves, "I cannot see evidence / proof of God's existence," but that does not give them the knowledge concerning other people's ability to see. Their blindness has no effect on whether or not God exists. Nor on whether or not other people can see evidence / proof for God's existence.

If I say, "I have seen proof of God's existence," there is no philosopher who can logically say that I do not know if God exists or not. They don't have my eyes, my progressions of thought, or my experiences. They don't know.

Nor can any philosopher say with logical integrity that God has not given humanity evidence / proof of his existence. All they can logically do is speak for themselves and say, "I cannot see what you see." Anything beyond that is nonsense.

Think again of the title of this book, *Has God Proven His Existence?* Philosophers or anyone else who answer, "No," are expressing their own ignorance.

Point 5.17: The God Who Selectively Reveals Himself

Now it is time to expose one last assumption (number 9) at the foundation of Western philosophy. There are many ways to state it but I will word it this way: **Western atheistic philosophers assume that God, if he exists, is fair.** By fair, I mean God treats everyone the same.

There are many ways in which God does treat everyone the same. However, God does not equally reveal himself and his works to everyone. Jesus explained this aspect of the character of God:

> *"I praise You, Father, Lord of heaven and earth, that You have hidden these things from the wise and intelligent and have revealed them to infants."*
> Matthew 11:25

Here, Jesus was talking about God revealing the reality of miracles and the reality of God's existence. Jesus spoke of this same concept in other Bible passages, as well, such as when he explained that people must be like little children to understand the things of God.[57]

The God of the Bible *selectively reveals himself and selectively hides himself.*

Western philosophy ignores this biblically-derived concept of God. Instead, the philosophers assume that if god reveals himself to one person then he is obligated to reveal himself to everyone. It is that assumption about the nature of god that leads the atheistic philosophers to reason that if god has not revealed himself to them, then god has not revealed himself to you or anyone else.

In reality, the God of Judaism and Islam also selectively hides himself. That means the God who is believed in by the majority of the world today selectively reveals himself.

Atheistic philosophers ignore or are ignorant of this fact. They are not talking about the God in whom the rest of the world believes. They have designed and engineered their own god. Then after all their study they declare, "God doesn't exist!" Well, I agree that their god does not exist. If that is the god they are talking about, then I too am an atheist. But the God revealed in the Bible is different than their god. He does exist. Let me tell you how I know.

Point 5.18: Who Are the Childlike?

If God reveals himself to infants, it is worth identifying who those infants are.

---

57 Matthew 18:3; Mark 10:15; Luke 18:17.

Where Does the Evidence Lead? Atheism or Theism?

Jesus encouraged his disciples to become like little children, but they obviously could not make themselves younger. Rather than referring to chronological age, Jesus was referring to having the characteristics of a child or to be childlike.

Jesus contrasted those childlike characteristics to those who were "wise and intelligent," but the context of his words was of people who thought of themselves as wise and intelligent. They knew better than to believe in miracles. Unlike children, they had become jaded and cynical with age.[58]

To be childlike is to be humble. Repeatedly the Bible writers talked about God giving grace to the humble. At the same time, they warned that God is opposed to the proud (I Peter 5:5; James 4:6). The God of the Bible actively resists and holds at arm's length those who are proud. This is a characteristic in the nature of God.

My wife, Linda, is a professional in child development and teaching. She describes the characteristic she most enjoys about children is the awe they show when learning. Rather than clinging to their already fixed thoughts, they are moldable, willing to exchange what they presently know with new information.

To be childlike is to be moldable, wide-eyed, awed by majestic splendor. When a child looks up at the stars, they posture themselves *under* the majesty of all that which is greater than themselves. Rather than exalting themselves as the master of what they see, children know they don't know. They are eager to learn and willing to change.

This is in contrast to those who have looked at the stars a thousand times and yawn at the site. They think they know all

---

58 This context is Matthew 11:20-25.

that needs to known, and now they are bored. They see nothing deserving their undivided attention, much less their awe. Nothing within them bows, yields, or calls for their respect. They stand firm and erect, humble before nothing, because they see nothing greater than themselves.

Similar distinctions between the childlike and the not-so-childlike can be identified when two people move their attention from the grandeur of the heavens to the smallest of creatures. One person may look through a microscope and be overwhelmed by the complexity of life in a single cell. Another person may look through the same microscope and see nothing that stands out as deserving of wonder. Instead of being like a child, the second person may posture themselves in a detached and arrogant attitude that says, "I am wise and intelligent." They scoff at the thought that anything beyond the natural could be at work within the living cell. All is natural, nothing is beyond the grasp of the human mind. Such a skeptical way of thinking is the opposite of the childlikeness which Jesus said is necessary to see the things of God.

Point 5.19: Move to Where You Can See God

Jesus encouraged his disciples to become like little children, implying that the characteristics of a child may be embraced by an act of their own will. How does this work?

Here is a comparison. My wife and I enjoy watching wildlife. One day she spotted a deer off in the distance, but when she pointed it out to me, I could not see it. After realizing there was a tree positioned directly between me and the deer, she asked me to move closer to her. As soon as I moved, I could clearly see the deer.

In a comparative way, we can say some people are positioned wrongly to see God. However, it is not a tree blocking their vision. It may be a progression of thought, detour questions, definitions of certain words, or something that disqualifies them from seeing God. In particular, God actively hides himself from people who are proud, cynical, and unwilling to learn. From that position, God cannot be seen. A person must move into a position of humility and wonder to see him.

This truth can only be understood by the person who is looking for the true God. A person who is looking for the philosophically-engineered concept of god will not understand. They are looking for a make-believe god for which there is no evidence / proof.

To see evidence / proof of the existence of the true God, a person needs to look for the God who hides himself from the proud and reveals himself to the childlike. Knowing this about the nature of the true God, they will move themselves into the proper position from where he can be seen.

Point 5.20: Blaise Pascal Said He Encountered God

Blaise Pascal (1623–1662), was a famous French mathematician and philosopher, who was often involved in his day with discussions about the existence of God. He explained that one night he had a deep encounter with God, after which he wrote these words:

> God of Abraham, God of Isaac, God of Jacob, not of
> the philosophers and the intellectuals. The God of
> Jesus Christ.[59]

---

59 Blaise Pascal. *Oeuvres Complètes*. (Paris: Seuil, 1960), p. 618; Pascal also wrote this in his celebrated *Pensées*.

This revelation about God was so profound to Pascal that he sewed a note with these words into the inner liner of his coat, and always transferred the note when he changed clothes. He never wanted to forget.

Pascal rejected the god who had been proposed by the philosophers and discovered the God who is revealed in the Bible.

Now consider if some atheistic philosopher ridicules Pascal for his claim that he encountered God.

On what basis is that philosopher ridiculing Pascal? Does that philosopher have the same progressions of thought that Pascal had? Does that philosopher have a progression of thought that opens his eyes to see God? Is that philosopher looking for the same God Pascal was looking for? Is that philosopher someone from whom God is hiding? Does that philosopher have any rational basis to reject what Pascal said about his encounter with God?

No. That philosopher is blind in many ways. All she can logically say is, "I have not encountered God, but it is possible that Pascal has."

This is another reason atheism is a position that cannot be held with logical integrity. Not only is it impossible to prove God's non-existence, but the God of Christianity, Judaism, and Islam selectively hides himself.

Point 5.21: Millions Have Seen!

I can't prove it, but I suspect most people on the earth—including most Christians, Jews, and Muslims—have had an experience of looking up into the stars at night and been stirred to worship the creator. It was their immediate reaction. As the Psalmist said,

> *The heavens are telling of the glory of God;*
> *And their expanse is declaring the work of His hands.*
>
> Psalm 9:1

Of course, the average person may worship God when first gazing at the stars, but ten minutes later allow their mind to shift into a different progression of thought and wonder if God is really responsible for the existence of those stars.

During the first few minutes they could see, but then a few minutes later they couldn't see. Why? Because they have one progression of thought that opens their eyes to see and another progression that blinds their eyes from seeing God. Furthermore, God reveals himself to the humble and hides himself from those who are not childlike.

Point 5.22: Are Answers to Prayer Evidence?

Finally, it is worth talking about the evidence / proof God gives of himself to those who have a relationship with him.

The Christian God wants relationships with people. This is the good news announced in the Bible. God not only revealed himself in Bible times, but he desires today to interact with people, answer their prayers, change their lives for the better, communicate with them, guide them, empower them, and share his life and love. This is not in accordance with the philosophically-derived concept of a transcendent god, but it is with the God revealed in the Bible.

You may or may not assign any credibility to theists who talk about God answering their prayers, but I do. This does not mean I believe every person who testifies about God answering their prayers. Many such reports can be easily explained as coincidences, active imaginations, wishful thinking, etc.

However, I have traveled the world and taught about God in more than 25 nations. Everywhere I have gone, theists have told me about prayers they have seen God answer and other works of God in their daily lives.

I have no real statistics to offer, but my experiences lead me to believe over half of all the Christians in the world have at least one testimony of God answering their prayers. Since there are about 2.2 billion Christians in the world, that means over 1 billion have accepted answers to prayer as evidence of God's existence.

Weighing the Evidence

Perhaps a large percentage of those Christians have confused the answer to a prayer with coincidences or imagined results. There are obviously some gullible people out there.

Where Does the Evidence Lead? Atheism or Theism?

But I also recognize that the vast majority of Christians are using something similar to the scientific method to understand how God answers prayer. They pray, watch to see if and when God answers, then try to understand which prayers God answers. In other words, they experiment, observe, form a hypothesis, test more, observe more, modify their hypothesis, and then experiment more. The truth is most Christians spend their entire life adjusting and modifying their prayer life (their hypotheses) in accordance with their best understanding of how God responds to them.

The seriousness of Christians in the pursuit of truth about this is most obvious when their prayers don't get answered. They often go through disillusionment or even a crisis of faith. Their reaction reveals how they were actually looking for verifiable results and did not get it. In other words, not all Christians are gullible or ignorant.

We could talk about why those Christians' prayers did not get answered the way they wanted, but that is the subject for a whole other book. It is a detour subject. The point to be taken here is that disillusionment with unanswered prayer is experienced by many theists at some time during their life, revealing how Christians are serious about pursuing truth about God's existence and understanding how he interacts with this world. Of course, atheists cannot accept even one report of God answering a prayer because of their assumption that God doesn't exist. Again, an assumption determines what an atheist will accept as credible. And basing such a belief on an assumption is to base it on nothing at all.

From the perspective of the theist, answers to prayer are evidence of God's existence. This adds to the truth that theists base their **faith** on what they have accepted as evidence. The atheists may not accept the same evidence, but to think theists don't build their **faith** on evidence is not true.

Point 5.23: The Benefits of a Bond with God

At the end of Section 4, we discussed how **faith** is similar to love in that it creates a bond. That bond allows life and strength to flow to the trusting individual.

We considered the example of athletes who have **faith** in their coach. Because of their **faith,** the coach is more effective in giving instructions and encouragement. We also considered students having **faith** in their teachers, resulting in the students accessing greater benefits from their teachers.

Similar dynamics are operating in relationships between God and people who have **faith** in God. They have a bond with God. Of course, atheistic philosophers cannot accept this because of their assumption that god doesn't exist and if he did exist, he would be transcendent. Dismissing those assumptions of the philosophers about god and looking for the God revealed in the Bible, we can consider the *benefits of a bond with God.*

BIBLICALLY-DERIVED UNDERSTANDING:
FAITH AND LOVE CREATE A BOND WITH GOD

That reference alone—benefits of a bond with God—ought to stop everyone in their tracks. People are typically impressed when someone says they are connected with a president, a famous sports figure, or a movie star. Yet, such connections are paltry compared to having a bond with God.

The God of the Bible is revealed as one who not only answers prayer but also puts his spirit within people. Through a spirit-to-spirit connection, God communicates, guides, empowers, frees people of sin, improves their life, and shares his life and love with those who have faith. Tens of thousands of books have been written about those benefits.

This is not the place to repeat what is written in all those books. What is essential is that any reader looking for evidence / proof of God needs to look for the real God, not the transcendent god of the philosophers and the intellectuals.

Point 5.24: Are Changed Lives Evidence?

Several years ago, I was in a meeting with about 100 Christians. The speaker asked individuals in the audience to stand up whenever he made a statement that was true in their life. Then he made statements such as:

1. I was an alcoholic, but since I became a Christian, I have been sober.
2. I had a sexual addiction, but since I became a Christian, I have experienced freedom in this area.
3. I had constant battles with anxiety and panic attacks, but since I became a Christian, those battles have ended.
4. I was bitter and filled with unforgiveness, but since I became a Christian, I have been able to forgive people.
5. I suffered from depression and suicidal thoughts, but since I became a Christian, I have no longer been tormented by those thoughts.

6. My spouse and I were on the verge of divorce, but since I became a Christian, our relationship dramatically improved.

7. I had a sickness that I could not get healed from, but since I became a Christian, I have been healed.

By the time the speaker finished making such statements, almost everyone in the room was standing. Of course, not everyone claiming to be free in one area was free in all areas but the fact that so many people had experienced at least one area of being set free was evidence to me that God exists and is working in the world.

A critic may credit such changes to something other than God, perhaps psychological changes associated with blind faith. Indeed, I can agree that there are other possible explanations. That is why I do not categorize such testimonies as proof. But to me, they still have some credibility as evidence.

WEIGHING THE EVIDENCE

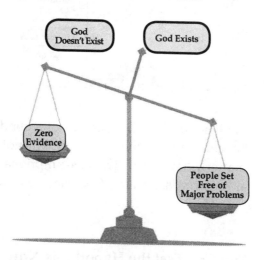

Where Does the Evidence Lead? Atheism or Theism?

I have traveled the world and discovered people everywhere will give testimonies to similar experiences concerning how God changed their life for the better. The sheer volume of such testimonies adds to the evidence for me.

Millions of people will testify to experiencing other benefits of their bond with God: his guidance, empowering, encouragement, comfort, assurance, inspiration, life, and love. They live every day with this evidence / proof of God's existence.

WEIGHING THE EVIDENCE

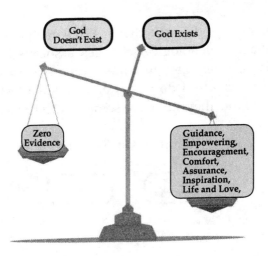

We could talk about the other benefits of a bond with God, but those who deny the existence of God will not accept the evidence no matter what we say. Their assumptions make them unable to hear our words. Besides, God may be hiding himself from them.

Point 5.25: You Can Test the Hypothesis Now

Atheists may ridicule the idea that God hides himself from

them, but remember they say, if God exists, he is hiding himself *from everyone*. Is their assumption more reasonable than the theist's hypothesis that God hides himself *from some people*?

The atheist's understanding is "an assumption" because it is impossible to test if God is hiding himself from everyone.

In contrast, the theist's understanding is a hypothesis. It can be tested, and I encourage you go ahead and test it for yourself.

TWO VIEWS OF GOD'S REVELATION OF HIMSELF

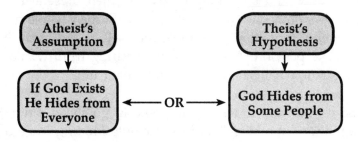

There is already some evidence available. Atheists like to point out how the most educated people are more likely to be atheists, while the less educated are more likely to be theists. That is a general observation, but if it is true, that offers some evidence that God hides himself from the wise and intelligent, while revealing himself to the childlike.

Rather than just accept that general observation, you can carry out a more exacting experiment to test the hypothesis yourself. If you are an atheist, who truly wants to know the truth, you can use the scientific method right now. If the hypothesis is true that God reveals himself to those who are childlike, then all you have to do is become childlike to see if God will reveal himself to you.

Where Does the Evidence Lead? Atheism or Theism?

What does that entail? As explained earlier, move from a position of thinking you are wise and intelligent and into a position of humility. Shift your mind out of a progression of thought that hides the evidence/proof of God's existence and into a progression that opens your eyes. Allow your mind to be moldable rather than fixed. Look for the Christian God, not the transcendent god of the philosophers.

The Christian God declared that he will reveal himself to all who seek him with their whole heart.[60] Someone seeking God with their whole heart would be willing to sacrifice their position, status, and admiration from others in order to find God. They would be willing to give up their present understanding. If someone truly seeks God with their whole heart, they would be willing to humble themselves and move into a childlike position. A person truly desiring truth would be willing to do what is necessary to gain that truth.

So if you want to test the hypothesis, go ahead. I did. So have millions of others. And he came out of hiding. We found him.

---

60 Recorded in several Bible passages, including Deuteronomy 4:29; Proverbs 8:17; Jeremiah 29:13.

Summary of Section Five

We followed the Western philosophical progression that leads to atheism / agnosticism. Along that progression we identified a series of assumptions. Most significantly, an assumption is required at the conclusion of that progression—the assumption of atheism. That requires the biggest blind leap.

THE WESTERN PHILOSOPHICAL PROGRESSION
LEADING TO ATHEISM / AGNOSTICISM

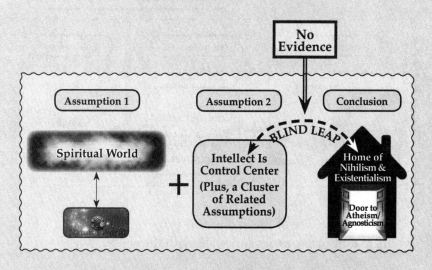

As we followed the Western philosophical progression we also realized that the philosophers are looking for a god they designed and engineered. I agree with the atheists that that god doesn't exist.

Where Does the Evidence Lead? Atheism or Theism?

The second progression of thought we followed leads to theism. Along that progression we identified hypotheses that can be tested. The results of that testing leads us to conclude those hypotheses are credible.

Furthermore, the second progression of thought leads to theism and that final step is supported by much evidence / proof.

THE PROGRESSION OF THOUGHT LEADING TO THEISM

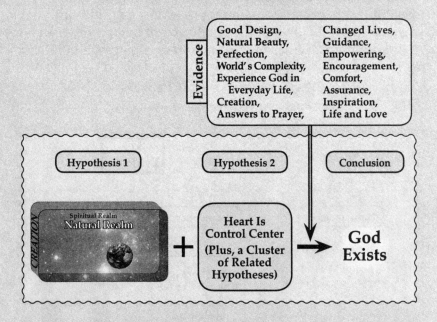

The God we see at the end of this progression is a God who wants to embrace people and walk with them.

Conclusion

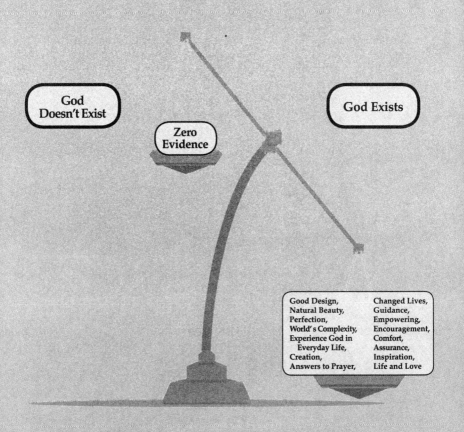

God Doesn't Exist

God Exists

Zero Evidence

Good Design, Natural Beauty, Perfection, World's Complexity, Experience God in Everyday Life, Creation, Answers to Prayer, Changed Lives, Guidance, Empowering, Encouragement, Comfort, Assurance, Inspiration, Life and Love

Acknowledgements

I want to thank the late Dr. Francis Schaeffer for first making me aware of the darkened path of Western philosophy. His book, *Escape from Reason,* started me down this road of study over thirty years ago.

I am also grateful for my friends who read through rough drafts of this book, offering their suggestions, corrections, and encouragement: Scott Stevens, Leon Kempt, Jason Rodriguez, Robin Rankin-Coffin, Roger Bennett, and Dr. Stan DeKoven. I chose my friends who each have an area of expertise related to a subject matter of this book.

James Bryson is the professional copy editor who has helped me on every writing project. Rev. Jerry Denton and Anthony Delatorre are my final proof readers.

Linda, my wife, has walked by my side for 40 plus years. She has carried my heart in her hand and prepared the path upon which I travel each day. She never stops working, caring for me and every other wandering soul along the way.

Linda, I am sorry when I have been obsessed with my work and stayed too long crafting my words or entangled with trivium. No one knows the days, weeks, and months you have had to share my heart with my computer. Others would be thanking you, rather than me, if they knew how often you have rightfully thought of my laptop as "the other woman."

Acknowledgements

Without Linda, my writing would be sterile and empty. As she rises each morning, the sun rises with her. My heart pivots to where she is moving. When I look at her, I smile for no reason. Linda picks me up when I am down and consistently surprises me with her graciousness. Indeed, she is evidence that God exists, and certainly, he must love me.

Appendix A
Glossary

The following terms have been defined as they are used in the body of this work.

Agnostic—
1. philosophical agnostic (the definition corresponding to Western philosophy): a person who believes that nothing is known or can be known of the existence or nature of God.[61]
2. common agnostic: a person who claims to not know if God exists or not.[62]

Atheist—a person who believes there is no God.[63]

Cosmology—one's understanding of the origin and nature of the world.

Confirmation bias—the tendency to interpret new evidence as confirmation of one's existing beliefs or theories.[64]

Deism—the belief in a God who created the world but is not involved with the world he created.

Dualistic—twofold, double, or dual.

---

61 Taken directly from the *Oxford English Dictionary*.
62 The distinctions between these two definitions are explained in points 1.19-1.20.
63 In some contexts distinctions are made concerning different types of atheism, but those distinctions are not made in this book.
64 Taken directly from the *Oxford Living Dictionary*.

Glossary

Enlightenment—18th-century movement marked by rationalism and the rejection of traditional social, religious, and political values.

Entropy—when used in the context of science, the gradual degradation or running down of all matter and energy into death and disorder.

Epistemology—the study focusing on the question, "How can we be certain that what we think is really true?"

Evangelical—short for Evangelical Christian; an Evangelical Christian is a Christian who believes the Bible is inspired by God and believes a person must be born again to be a Christian.[65]

Evidence—
1. the available body of facts or information indicating whether a belief or proposition is true or valid.[66]
2. definition as used when contrasting to proof: facts pointing to a certain conclusion, but not eliminating all doubt.

Existentialism—20th century, philosophical movement in which the individual is identified as totally responsible to create his or her own meaning for existence.

Faith—
1. definition corresponding to Western Philosophy: a mental assent to certain ideas, especially religious ideas, for which there is no evidence.
2. definition corresponding to individuals who wrote the Bible: confidence and conviction in the heart of a person, resulting from evidence that has been deemed credible.

---

65 The word, Evangelical, is used in many different ways in different contexts. The definition offered here is common among secular people in the US, and this is how the word is used in this book.
66 Taken directly from the *Oxford Living Dictionary*.

Fallen—definition as used in the context of human nature as understood in Evangelical Christianity: corrupt and subject to sin as a result of the sin of Adam and Eve.

Hope—definition as used in the context of religion: an expectation and desire within the heart for a certain event to happen.

Hypothesis—a proposed explanation made on the basis of limited evidence as a starting point for further investigation.[67]

Natural theology—the study of God derived from studying nature, rather than knowledge derived from special revelation, such as the Bible or personal experience.

Nihilism—the view that traditional values and beliefs are unfounded and that existence is senseless and useless.[68]

Philosophy—the study of theories of such things as the meaning of life, knowledge, and belief.

Proof—
1. evidence or argument establishing a fact or the truth of a statement.[69]
2. definition as used when contrasting to evidence: facts pointing to a certain conclusion and eliminating all doubt.

Rationalism—belief that values and actions should be based on reason and knowledge rather than on religious belief or an emotional response.

Revealed theology—thoughts about God based on revelation, such as that revealed in Scripture or religious experience.

---

67 Taken directly from the *Oxford Living Dictionary*.
68 Taken directly from *Merriam Webster Dictionary*.
69 Taken directly from the *Oxford Living Dictionary*.

Glossary

Scientific method—the systematic pursuit of knowledge through the collection of data through observation and experimentation, and the formulation of hypotheses.

Secular—denoting attitudes, activities, or other things that have no religious basis.

Theism—belief in the existence of God, especially a belief in one God who created and is involved with creation.

Transcendent—beyond, separated, unreachable, unknowable.

Appendix B
Questions for Discussion

Section One

Progression of Thought Leading to Atheism / Agnosticism

pt. 1.1: Have you had an epistemological discussion recently?
If so, about what? With whom?

pt. 1.2: Have you heard about Socrates before this?
What do you remember about Socrates?

pt. 1.3: In addition to the cosmology of the big bang theory and
a literal interpretation of Genesis 1, can you identify
any other cosmology that some people hold?
Why is Plato's cosmology considered dualistic?
Imagine for a moment Plato's understanding that every
deep thought you have is actually reaching into and
experiencing the spiritual world of thoughts. Does
that seem reasonable to you?

pt. 1.4: Does Aristotle's Prime Mover sound like the God of the
Bible?
If so, in what ways? In what ways does the Prime Mover
sound different than the God of the Bible?

pt. 1.5: Do you keep aware and up to date with any progression
of thought that is developing in some other field?

pt. 1.6: How did Augustine make Plato's cosmology more accept-
able to Christians?

Questions for Discussion

Were people in the Middles who followed Augustine's teaching that faith is to believe what the Church teaches, really Christians?

Augustine taught that the human intellect and heart are fallen, while Aquinas taught that humans are able to arrive at truth with their intellect independently of their heart. Who do you think was correct?

pt. 1.7: Before Copernicus' book was published about the earth revolving around the sun, what did most people in Europe believe about this subject?

Those who fully embraced the Scientific Revolution came to believe that the world runs according to natural laws instead of spiritual beings controlling the world. What do you believe about this?

Why did thoughts about spiritual beings controlling the world hinder people from understanding the world?

pt. 1.8: The fathers of the Scientific Revolution still saw the Church as the source of truth about God. Do you think people around you today still look to the Church as that source of truth?

Do you ever form a hypothesis about how the world works and then test to see if the hypothesis is true? If so, give an example.

pt. 1.9: Do you agree with the idea that the things of faith cannot be known with certainty?

Do you agree that faith is the acceptance of ideas without any evidence?

pt. 1.10: Plato's dualistic cosmology still lies at the foundation of Western philosophy. Does it still lie at the foundation of your worldview?

Questions for Discussion

pt. 1.11: When you think of the Enlightenment, do you tend to think it was positive or negative?

Do you know someone who is a deist?

Do you know someone who is an atheist?

pt. 1.12: Do you think natural theology is able to offer evidence of God's existence?

In Romans 1:20, the apostle Paul talked about creation as evidence of God nature. Do you see creation as evidence of God's existence?

pt. 1.13: Do you agree with Kant that the spiritual world is transcendent, in the sense that the spiritual world is totally separate and unreachable?

Why did Kant's thinking change philosophy so much?

Have you been exposed to teachers who see the spiritual and natural worlds as totally separated? If so, when and where?

pt. 1.14: Do you believe God will reveal himself to you if you take a blind leap into his arms?

pt. 1.15: When Friedrich Nietzsche declared that God is dead, do you think he was he saying he did not believe in God?

Have you heard anyone ridiculing faith in God?

Do you know someone who says there is no spiritual world?

pt. 1.16: Which of the following three aspects of the philosophical progression seem correct to you:

   a. starting with Plato's cosmology
   b. creating a greater and great separation between the spiritual and natural worlds
   c. labeling the spiritual world transcendent meaning, separate and unreachable

Questions for Discussion

pt. 1.17: Why is it that the philosophical progression can only lead to the front door of atheism /agnosticism?
Why does it always require a blind leapt to become an atheist?
Atheists often say they will not accept anything without evidence. It that true?

pt. 1.18: What is the difference between evidence for God's existence and reasons to become an atheist?
Have you ever felt pressured to become an atheist /agnostic?

pt. 1.19: Why is philosophical agnosticism not a logically defensible view?
What assumption must be made to embrace philosophical agnosticism?

pt. 1.20: Do you know anyone who holds to common agnosticism rather than philosophical agnosticism?
Why do some people prefer to hold to philosophical agnosticism rather than common agnosticism?

Section Two

The Values of Atheism /Agnosticism

pt. 2.1: Have you ever felt like you were standing at the door of decision about atheism or agnosticism?
Is so, do you think at the time you had all the information you needed to make an informed decision?

pt. 2.2: If you were to change from theist to atheist, how would your values change about:
   a. marriage?
   b. commitment to marriage?
   c. sex?
   d. abortion?
   e. euthanasia?

Questions for Discussion

If nothing is sacred how would you feel about
  a. jokes about God?
  b. jokes about other religions?
Why do you think Muslims are so protective of the Koran?
Is anything sacred? If so, what?

pt. 2.3: What do you think is the purpose or function of religion?
Have you experienced oppression from religion?

pt. 2.4: Is there right and wrong? If so, on what basis can we
determine what is right and what is wrong?
Do you think sin and guilt are absolute?

pt. 2.5: How are the modern-day attitudes about sex outside
of marriage tied to the historical philosophical progression?
Do you ever feel a battle going on within you between
your familial, traditional, and religious values versus
the values of the people around you?
If so, what is the strongest battle for you?

pt. 2.6: Were your parents, grandparents, or great grandparents
part of the cultural revolution of the 1960s? How
did it affect them?
In what way was the cultural revolution of the 1960's the
result of philosophy?
What cultural revolution do you see happening around
you today? What is the thinking behind it?
Consider the value embraced by adults living in the 1950s
to not tell others about their problems so as to not
make other people carry their pain. Is that a modern
value? How have things changed?

pt. 2.7: What north star is helping you make decisions today?
Is there a north star that influences your behavior, but you

Questions for Discussion

really don't embrace that north star as your most
important guidance point?

pt. 2.8: Can people be good?
Can we trust them to live good?

pt. 2.9: Are there good and evil people?
Are murderers evil? Are thieves evil?
How has society's views of others changed in the last
70 years?
What is "life" according to theists versus atheists?
Is there any sacred element to love?
Is there any sacred element to sex?

pt. 2.10: Have you ever experienced despair oriented around an
awareness that your life has no meaning?
How are the thoughts of nihilism similar to the thoughts
of depression?
Does your life have meaning?
If so, from where do you derive meaning to your life?

pt. 2.11: Do you feel responsible to create your own meaning for
your life?
Are you living authentically?
Is there value in living authentically?
Is living authentically the north star in your life?
If you can draw no meaning for your own life from God,
is it worth living?
Do you draw meaning from God? If so, what meaning?

pt. 2.12: What is the a difference between the throne inherent
in atheistic teachings versus the throne Christians refer
to when they talk about reigning with Jesus?

Questions for Discussion

Section Three
Exchanging Assumptions with Hypotheses

pt. 3.1: Did Plato have proof of the spiritual world that he envisioned?
In what way is your cosmology similar to Plato's cosmology?

pt. 3.2: Were you previously aware of how the Bible portrays the heavens and earth within creation?

pt. 3.3: Are you right now in God's presence?
Can people who live on the other side of the earth look up and be oriented toward God's throne?

pt. 3.4: According to Colossians 1:16-17, what would happen if Jesus was not exercising authority over creation?
According to Job 34:14-15, is God's Spirit within every living human being?
What is the difference between a cosmology with two worlds versus one with two realms?

pt. 3.5: What do you think about Paul's intellectual ability compared to Plato's?
If someone believes they should build their worldview on Plato's dualistic cosmology, shouldn't they also build their worldview on the other fundamental aspects of his cosmology, such as his explanation that there are only four elements, (air, earth, fire, and water) and these elements are structured as four polygons (the tetrahedron, cube, octahedron, and icosahedron)? Plato mentioned a fifth polygon (the dodecahedron) and said the gods used it for arranging the constellations. Should we also build on that aspect of his cosmology?

Questions for Discussion

pt. 3.6: Is your cosmology more like Plato's or Paul's cosmology? Does it make any difference in daily life?

pt. 3.7: Consider the statement, "He who frames the argument wins the argument." Is it true?
Does starting the argument by assuming Plato's cosmology predetermine the conclusion of the argument?

pt. 3.8: Was Plato's exclusion of God from the natural world any more than an assumption?
Does Paul's cosmology seem more or less reasonable than Plato's cosmology?

pt. 3.9: Have you ever heard of any philosophy student questioning Plato's cosmology? Or do they just assume it?
Have you had any experiences that seem impossible to explain with only the known natural laws that govern the natural world?

pt. 3.10: Do you live your life in accordance with the idea that the intellect is the control center of human nature?
Do you agree with Aquinas that your mind is able to arrive at truth independently of your heart?
If someone accepts the ancient Greek philosophical understanding of human nature that the rational part of our being should reign, shouldn't they also accept the ancient Greek philosophical understanding that human behavior is regulated by blood, phlegm, and black and yellow bile?

pt. 3.11: How much credibility do you put in Jesus' words as recorded in the Bible about the words and actions of people proceeding from the heart?
Can you imagine any situation in which a person is controlled by some aspect of their nature other than their heart or intellect?

Questions for Discussion

pt. 3.12: Why is it difficult to build on Plato's cosmology and at the same time conceive of human nature integrated in the spiritual and natural realms?
When you envision the human soul, do you envision it as the same shape and size as the physical body?

pt. 3.13: What differences can you discern between the functions of your heart and the functions of your head?

pt. 3.14: Can you come up with an example of how love influences the thoughts of a person?
Can you come up with an example of how unforgiveness influences the thoughts of a person?
Can you remember a time when you realized your thoughts were being distorted by issues of your heart?

pt. 3.15: In what circumstances should you trust your intellect to arrive at truth independently of your heart?
In what circumstances should you not trust your intellect to arrive at truth independently of your heart?

pt. 3.16: In the example of Devin and Sean do you think they were each aware of how their hearts were guiding their questions?
Do you think Devin and Sean each considered themselves logical?

pt. 3.17: Can you think of a question that you were asked that was biased?
At the time it was asked, did you recognize that the question was designed to make you chase a bone?

pt. 3.18: Have you been involved in a discussion where critical thinking was used to steer you in the direction of the leader's bias?

Questions for Discussion

pt. 3.19: What is meant by "corollary concepts?"

Can you think of a case in which "a progression of thought is logical but the conclusion is not true?"

Have you been taught that questions are neutral and innocent?

pt. 3.20: Do you think a philosophy teacher knows ahead of time what answers the students will come up with to answer his questions?

Which students in a philosophy classroom will be most likely to argue fervently?

Which students in a philosophy classroom will be most likely to stay silent?

How many students in a philosophy classroom realize they are chasing bones?

Why is it that "asking the tough questions" can be deceptive?

pt. 3.21: Can a progression of thought that is logical lead to a false conclusion?

Can you think of two other questions that are not innocent or neutral?

pt. 3.22: If you found a book with over 1,000 pages of written instructions on how to build a robot would you conclude that someone must be responsible for writing that book?

Is it reasonable to conclude that a human being, with 100 trillion cells and each cell having a genetic code consisting of three billion letters, was the product of chance, with no outside intelligent input?

pt. 3.23: Do you think you have ever been deceived by a series of biased questions?

Do you think grade school teachers ever ask their students biased questions in accordance with a hidden agenda?

Do you ever question the questions that are asked of you?

Questions for Discussion

pt. 3.24: Do you think at least one new progression of thought is added into your brain everyday?

Can you think of a progression of thought that is in your brain but you wish it wasn't there?

Can you think of a time when a major life-changing event led to a major shift in your thinking?

pt. 3.25: Can you think of any progression of thought in your brain that is actually hindering you from seeing certain things?

Can you think of a progression of thought that you were taught that is enabling you to see things that you could not see previously?

pt. 3.26: Can you think of any area in which you have switched from one progression of thought to another in order to deal with a situation differently?

Are you thankful for all the progressions of thought you learned through your formal education?

pt. 3.27: How far down the historical philosophical progression of thought you are at? Is that because of the way you were raised, religious training, education, or something else?

Can you think of another question that is used to detour people away from the question, "Does God exist?"

Have you ever tried talking to someone with several detour questions in their mind? Was it productive?

pt. 3.28: In what ways does Christianity teach God is accessible? Could a person who embraces the philosophical progression be blind to those ways of God's accessibility?

pt. 3.29: Are you biased?

Do you design questions to guide yourself where you want to go?

Questions for Discussion

pt. 3.30: Are you logical?
  Do you enjoy listening to someone who is convinced
    they are right?
  Are people who think differently than you illogical?

pt. 3.31: Have you been choosing which progressions of thought
    are true by how logical they sound?
  Why do we need some basis other than the logic of the
    progression to decide which progressions of thought
    are true?
  Can you think of any other basis (other than examining
    assumptions, examining the heart, and examining
    the supporting evidence) upon which we can
    decide which progressions of thought are true?
  Do you understand the intellect or the heart to be the
    control center of human nature?

pt. 3.32: Can you think of someone whom you admire and who
    helped fashion your thoughts?
  Have you ever experienced your thoughts orienting
    in the opposite direction of someone with whom
    you were angry?
  Have you ever found yourself making a decision
    diametrically opposed to your father's decision?
  Have you ever felt disloyal to someone when you
    abandoned their way of thinking?

pt. 3.33: Are you cautious about listening to angry people?
  Why would anger or disappointment with one's father
    influence a person's concept of God?

pt. 3.34: Do you feel like guilt or shame could be strong enough
    motivations to alter one's view of God?
  Do you feel sexual passions could influence one's view
    of God?
  Do you think people consider the implications upon
    their sexual life before they become theists?

pt. 3.35: Do you think unrestrained pride could distort someone's thought processes?
Are you aware of ever being deceived by your own
pride?
Are you cautious when you are around prideful people?

pt. 3.36: Can you think of any other reason why someone may
want to be an atheist?
Do you think it is a difficult decision for someone to
become an atheist?
Do you think it is a difficult decision for someone to
become a theist?

Section Four

What Is Faith?

pt. 4.1: Do most of the people around you consider the intellect
or the heart as the control center of their being?
Do most of the people around you think of the intellect
or the heart as the seat of faith?

pt. 4.2: Can you think of any group of people who think in
relational terms rather than abstract terms?
Can you be comfortable thinking of faith as trust?

pt. 4.3: Was setting faith and knowledge up as opposing
concepts a rationally justified step?
Was it rationally justifiable to define faith as mental
assent to certain ideas without evidence?
Can faith be based on evidence and still be faith?

pt. 4.4: Which understanding of faith, that of the Bible writers
or that of the Western philosophers, came first?

Questions for Discussion

About what time in history did the understanding of faith, as mental ascent to ideas without evidence, develop?

pt. 4.5: Have you ever experienced an increase in faith as a result of hearing or reading?

pt. 4.6: If faith results from hearing, reading, seeing, or experiencing, how is faith different than knowing?
Have you ever come to believe in something after having an experience?

pt. 4.7: Can you think of something of which you became convinced was credible, but you still did not put your faith in it?
Can you think of something of which you became convinced was credible and then you put your faith in it?

pt. 4.8: Do you know someone who is a theist who claims to have faith in God but they actually have not based their faith on evidence?
Do you know an atheist who thinks all theists are insane?

pt. 4.9: Have you ever heard someone take a Bible verse totally out of context and say it means something which the author never meant to say?
Assuming God does exist, does it make sense that he would bless people for making irrational decisions such as killing their own child?

pt. 4.10: If Soren's understanding of faith is wrong, why do you suppose atheists seized upon his understanding of faith?
If faith is conviction and assurance, how could it be based on no evidence?

Questions for Discussion

pt. 4.11: Have you ever listened to two people argue when they had different definitions of key words? If so, were they productive?

pt. 4.12: What percentage of your knowledge do you think came to you as a result of being taught and deducing ideas from that taught knowledge?
Have you ever seen an atom? Do you believe in atoms?

pt. 4.13: Concerning what subject do your consider your parents very credible sources?
How much credibility do you assign to your physician?
How much credibility do you assign to college professors?
How much credibility do you assign to the news media?

pt. 4.14: Have you ever looked at a list of proposed errors in the Bible?
Have you ever studied a scholarly study refuting those proposed errors?
If you were reading a science text book and found an error in it, would you discard that book?

pt. 4.15: If you had 27 books on your library shelf, all from the first century and all talking about one famous individual, wouldn't you give those books some credibility?

pt. 4.16: Do you know of any secular (nonreligious) book that has accurately predicted the time and place of someone's birth and death?
Have you ever seen any of the Dead Sea Scrolls?

pt. 4.17: How important is your faith to you?
Does your faith influence how you spend your money?

pt. 4.18: Do you have a strong bond with someone like a coach, mentor, or teacher?

Questions for Discussion

If so, what do you gain from the relationship?
Have you ever experienced the breaking of a trusting relationship? If so, what did you experience? What did you lose?

Section Five

Where Does the Evidence Lead? Atheism or Theism?

pt. 5.1: The historic philosophical progression is built on at least the six assumptions mentioned here. Doesn't that seem absurd for philosophers who study logic and claim to be the most logical elite among us?
Atheism assumes God does not exist. Can you think of any other field of study in which the academics allow their entire system of thought to be built on such a huge, underlying assumption?

pt. 5.2: If you catch a four-year-old with cookie crumbs around his mouth, do you have evidence or proof that that four-year-old ate the cookies?
Even if none of the five things mentioned "prove" to you that God exists, do any of these things point to or suggest a creator? Good design? Natural beauty? Perfection? Complexity of the universe? Experience of God in everyday life?

pt. 5.3: Do atheists have any proof/evidence that the experiences theists claim were from God are not true?
Is it rational for atheists to reject all the testimonies of theists about their experiences with God?
Do you reject all the testimonies theist's give of experiencing God?
Have you had any experience that proves, points to, or suggests a creator's existence?

Questions for Discussion

pt. 5.4: How much evidence on one side does it take to outweigh no evidence on the other side?

Do you give any weight to the five things theists point to as evidence?

pt. 5.5: Previous to reading this, did you think theists base their decision to believe in God on no evidence?

Previous to reading this, did you think atheists base their decision to disbelieve in God on evidence?

How have your thoughts changed on these issues?

pt. 5.6: Taking into account what we know about the physical forces that govern the world, does it seem logical to you that the world has always existed?

Have you met anyone who changed from atheist to theist after learning about the big bang theory?

pt. 5.7: How do you suppose the philosophical idea that God will not reveal himself irrefutably is linked to the philosophical idea that faith is to accept an idea without evidence?

pt. 5.8: Were there only a few people in the Bible who were shown to have experienced irrefutable proof of God's existence?

pt. 5.9: Is there a difference between coercing knowledge of God's existence and coercing faith in God?

Do you know anyone who says God revealed himself to them in an irrefutable way?

Do you know anyone who says God coerced them to have faith in him?

Even if God proves his existence to a person, God may still woo that person to himself with love. Why?

Questions for Discussion

pt. 5.10: Do you think people before the Enlightenment accepted creation as proof of God's existence because they were not as smart as people are today?
Is it rational to say God cannot or will not prove his existence?

pt. 5.11: For you, is a watch proof of the existence of a watchmaker?
For you, is a car proof of the existence of a car maker?
For you, is the world proof of the existence of a world maker?

pt. 5.12: Are you skeptical of the atheistic philosopher's judgement?
Can you develop a progression of thought that leads you to doubt your own existence?
If you did develop a progression of thought that led you to doubt your own existence, would that progression influence whether or not you exist?

pt. 5.13: Can you think of something that was labeled "a mystery" and, as a result, you stopped trying to figure it out?
Do you think there are any progressions of thought in your mind that are blinding you from seeing certain physical realities? If so, can you give an example?

pt. 5.14: There are two possibilities mentioned. Can you think of a third possibility that explains why students lose their faith?
Which of the two possibilities is most reasonable to you?

pt. 5.15: Do you have any training that opens your eyes to see something most other people cannot see?
Does that training hinder you from seeing anything? If so, what?

Questions for Discussion

pt. 5.16: Have you ever had someone tell you, "You can't know if God exists?"
Can anyone logically say to you, "You can't know if God exists?"

pt. 5.17: How many assumptions that we have not talked about do you supposed are at the foundation of the philosophical progression leading to atheism / agnosticism?
How many assumptions can you think of that are at the foundation of the progression leading to theism?
Do you have any personal experiences that lead you to believe God selectively reveals himself?

pt. 5.18: Do you want to see evidence for the existence of God?
If, indeed, God does selectively reveal himself as explained here, what do you have to do to see evidence / proof for his existence?

pt. 5.19: Can you become like a child by an act of your will?
Do you think you are positioned in a place from where you can see God?

pt. 5.20 Have you ever looked for the philosophically-derived god?
Have you ever looked for the "God of Abraham, God of Isaac, God of Jacob, not of the philosophers and the intellectuals?"
Why do you suppose Pascal sewed that patch on the inner lining of his coat?

pt. 5.21: Have you ever looked up at the heavens and started praising God?
Have you ever experienced a transition in your thoughts in which you first were acknowledging God's existence and then later were not?

237

Questions for Discussion

Did your changing thoughts have any effect on whether or not God exists?

pt. 5.22: Have you ever been convinced God answered one of your prayers?

If so, did you later on forget about it or change your mind and start believing God didn't answer your prayer? If so, why did you change? Did the changing of your mind have any influence on whether or not God actually did answer your prayer?

pt. 5.23: How many people do you think you are bonded to right now?

Do you benefit from those bonds? If so, how?

pt. 5.24: Do you have reason to believe your life has been changed for the better as a result of a bond with God?

Do you know other people who credit God with any dramatic changes in their life?

pt. 5.25: Have you noticed if the "wise and intelligent" are the most likely to deny God's existence? Is it possible that God is hiding himself from them?

Have you noticed that humble, childlike people are more likely to believe in God? Is it possible that God is revealing himself to them?

Father-Son Theology
Systematic Theology for the 21st Century Believer
Foreword by Dr. C. Peter Wagner

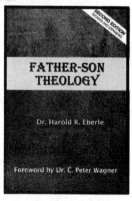

This is a complete systematic theology (900 pages), based on understanding God as Father and ourselves as children of God. *Father-Son Theology* offers a serious attempt to separate biblical Christianity from Western culture. This means:

1. Separating Christianity from the dualism that lies at the foundation of Western civilization
2. Eliminating the influence of Plato that came into the Church primarily through Augustine
3. Embracing a Hebraic/relational understanding of Scripture

Dr. Eberle considers this his most important work.

Thy Kingdom Come

The gospel Jesus and His disciples preached is not what we preach today. They preached, "Repent, for the Kingdom of God is at hand." We preach, "You are a sinner; Jesus died for your sins, and if you accept Jesus as Savior, you will be saved."

Why are these two gospels different? Who might be closer to the truth? Let's revisit Jesus' gospel and understand how to truly bring people into God's Kingdom.

Releasing Kings
For Ministry in the Marketplace
By John S. Garfield and Harold R. Eberle

"Kings" are what we call Christian leaders who have embraced the call of God upon their lives to work in the marketplace and from that position transform society. This book explains how marketplace ministry will operate in your community in concert with local churches and pastors. It provides a Scriptural basis for the expansion of the Kingdom of God into all areas of society.

Additional Books By Harold R. Eberle

Christianity Unshackled
Are You a Truth Seeker?

Most Christians in the Western world have no idea how profoundly their beliefs have been influenced by their culture. What would Christianity be like if it was separated from Western thought? After traveling the world and untangling the Western traditions of the last 2,000 years of Church history, Harold Eberle offers a Christian worldview that is clear, concise, and liberating. This will shake you to the core and then leave you standing on a firm foundation!

The Complete Wineskin
(Fourth edition)

The Body of Christ is in a reformation. God is pouring out His Holy Spirit, and our wineskins must be changed to handle the new wine. Will the Church come together in unity? How does the anointing of God work, and what is your role? What is the 5-fold ministry? How are apostles, prophets, evangelists, pastors, and teachers going to rise and work together? Where do small group meetings fit in? This book puts into words what you have been sensing in your spirit. (Eberle's best seller, translated into many languages, distributed worldwide.)

Grace...the Power to Reign
The Light Shining from Romans 5-8

We struggle against sin and yearn for God's highest. Yet, on a bad day, it is as if we are fighting against gravity. Questions go unanswered:

•Where is the power to overcome temptations?

•Is God really willing and able to breathe into us so that our dry bones can live and we can stand strong?

For anyone who has ever struggled to live godly, here are the answers.

God's Leaders for Tomorrow's World

You sense the call to leadership, but questions persist: "Does God want me to rise up? Do I truly know where to lead others? Is this pride? How can I influence people?" Through an understanding of leadership dynamics, learn how to develop godly charisma. Confusion will melt into order when you see the God-ordained lines of authority. Fear of leadership will change to confidence as you learn to handle power struggles. It is time to move into your "metron," that is, your God-given sphere of authority.

Leader Shifting

Turning a Church Over from One Senior Leader to Another

Leader Shifting can be glorious or gruesome, successful or fraught with mistakes that result in devastating lives. Success requires understanding basic relational and authority dynamics, then following well-thought out steps for a smooth succession.

Jesus Came Out of the Tomb... So Can You!

Forgiveness of sins is at the cross. Power over sin is in the resurrection and ascension. Yet, most Christians have no idea how to access the benefits of our Lord's resurrection and ascension. They are locked into death-centered Christianity rather than life-centered Christianity. This book empowers the reader to make the transition and "come out of the tomb."

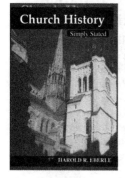

Church History, Simply Stated

How did the Church get to where She is today? How did we get so many denominations? Who were the leaders who formed our thoughts? Where is the Church going? To fully answer these questions requires a knowledge of the past. Here is a simple, concise explanation of Church history. With two or three hours of reading, anyone can develop a clear picture of our Christian heritage.

Additional Books By Harold R. Eberle

Precious in His Sight
A Fresh Look at the Nature of Humanity
(Third edition)

How evil are we? How can I love myself if I am evil? What happened when Adam sinned? How does that sin influence us? Where do babies go when they die? This book has implications upon our understanding of sin, salvation, who God is, evangelism, and how we live the victorious Christian life.

Developing a Prosperous Soul
Vol. I: How to Overcome a Poverty Mind-set
Vol. II: How to Move into God's Financial Blessings

There are fundamental changes you can make in the way you think, which will help you release God's blessings. This is a balanced look at the promises of God with practical steps you can take to move into financial freedom. It is time for Christians to recapture the financial arena. These two volumes will inspire and create faith in you to fulfill God's purpose for your life.

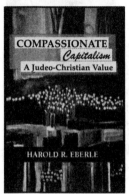

Compassionate Capitalism
A Judeo-Christian Value

As you read this book, you will learn how capitalism first developed as God worked among the Hebrew people in the Old Testament. The resulting economic principles then transformed Western society as they spread with Christianity. However, our present form of capitalism is different than that which God instilled in Hebrew society. What we need to do now is govern capitalism wisely and apply the principles of capitalism with compassion.

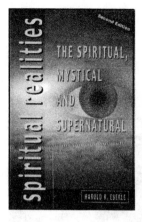

The Spiritual, Mystical, and Supernatural

The first five volumes of Harold R. Eberle's series of books entitled, *Spiritual Realities*, have been condensed into this one volume, 372 pages in length. Topics include how the spiritual and natural worlds are related, angelic and demonic manifestations, signs and wonders, miracles and healing, the anointing, good or evil spiritual practices, how people are created by God to access the spiritual realm, how the spirits of people interact, how people sense things in the spirit realm, and much more.

Victorious Eschatology
By Harold R. Eberle and Martin Trench
(Second edition)

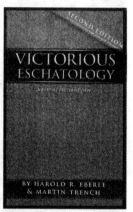

A biblically-based, optimistic view of the future. Along with a historical perspective, this book offers a clear understanding of Matthew 24, the book of Revelation, and other key passages about the events to precede the return of Jesus Christ. Satan is not going to take over this world. Jesus Christ is Lord and He will reign until every enemy is put under His feet!

On-line Bible College

- Independent or group study
- Earn a certificate, associates degree,
  or bachelors degree
- Audit courses
- Study and proceed at your own rate
- Sensibly priced

http://instituteforhopeandlife.com